INTERNSHIP GUIDE TO

Criminal Justice & Criminology

BUILDING PROFESSIONALISM THROUGH THEORY & PRACTICE

Pete Lopez, Ph.D. Armando J. Abney, Ph.D. Patricio Jaramillo, Ph.D.

Kendall Hunt
publishing company

Kendall Hunt
publishing company

www.kendallhunt.com
Send all inquiries to:
4050 Westmark Drive
Dubuque, IA 52004-1840

ISBN 978-1-5249-0155-4

Printed in the United States of America

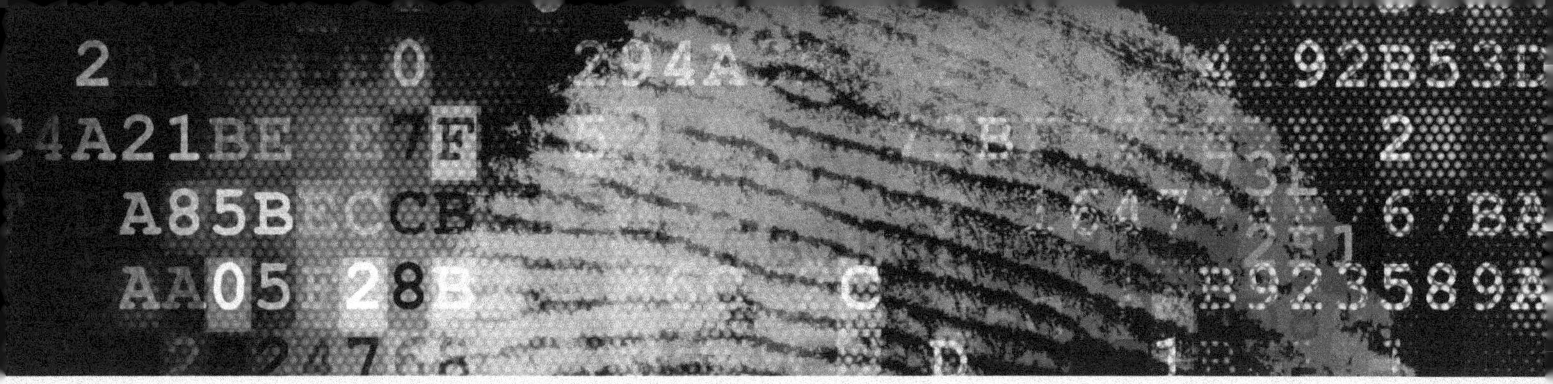

Table of Contents

Foreword

In *Internship Guide to Criminal Justice and Criminology*, Lopez, Abney, and Jaramillo have penned an essential text for those interested in obtaining *praxis* in criminal justice careers: merging years of "theory" into the development of an ongoing career of practice in the field. They focus on the critical *skills* needed for the fine art of moving from theory to practice (praxis) in a field at times overburdened by the first, and underrepresented by the latter.

In this latest text, designed to guide both faculty and students in developing a meaningful and practical system for deciding how to go about moving from the theory of the classroom to the practice of the critical skill sets in the criminal justice field, Lopez, Abney, and Jaramillo draw upon real-world experience in the justice system and in guiding graduates from university success to real-world success in their chosen justice fields.

The most critical sections of their *Internship Guide* are the 10 highly useful and well-thought out "Self-Reflection" assignments, designed to guide carefully the internship participant (and in no small degree the internship coordinators at both the university and the professional end of the internship process) in connecting the multiple and often conflicting "needs" and "solutions" of the internship process into a coherent and manageable "whole" producing graduates well prepared for the challenges that await them as practitioners.

As a practitioner and a former educator, I have found that the missing link for most new graduates frequently is an inability to apply thoughtfully the often conflicting requirements of theory (taught reliably well in our colleges and universities) with the *practice* needed in the field, that is, a *practical* application of theory. In my experience as a chief executive of a criminal justice-related consulting organization, many university criminal justice programs fail in this one critical area: problem solving. Most real-life criminal justice problem-solving ventures require the self-same reflection outlined in *Internship Guide*.

Lopez, Abney, and Jaramillo offer the field a unique and exciting solution to the frequently confronted dual problems of graduates who lack the practical skills necessary in the field, and, perhaps worse, graduates who make career choices that eventually turn out to be the wrong choice (due to a lack of supervised introductions to the true "life in the field"). Were more students introduced to the process of "self-Reflection" evidenced in *Internship Guide*, it would be a benefit to both the field and the thousands of new graduates produced annually by America's criminal justice and criminology programs.

James D. Ginger, PhD
CEO
Public Management Resources

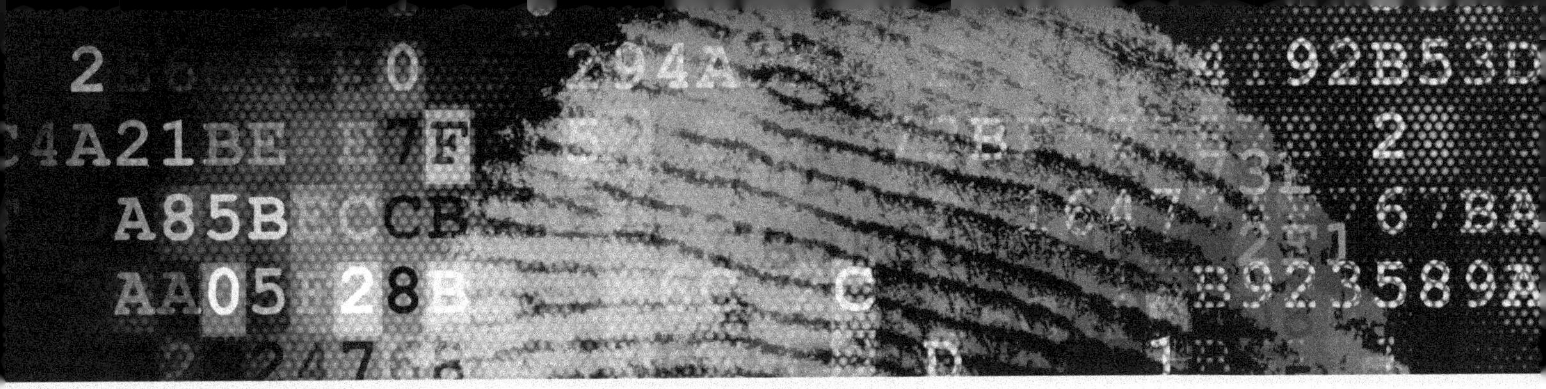

Preface

This book is written specifically for students enrolled in a criminal justice or criminology internship or practicum course. As a common practice, these courses usually require that students fulfill a specific number of hours of work experience in a criminal justice or related social service agency. In general, their purpose is to introduce students to real-world professional experiences. Although these experiences differ from the traditional classroom setting, their importance should not be underestimated. One of the purposes of these internship experiences is to give students an opportunity to apply academic training and related theory while engaged in professional practice. As such, these courses offer an important link between the students' academic training and the professional field they will eventually enter. In this regard, these experiences can fulfill important academic training goals and assist students in the selection of a profession that attracts their interest. Therefore, internship experiences can provide students with insights into their future careers and give them the opportunities to learn about professional standards related to their fields of interest. These standards include but are not limited to learning professional responsibilities, learning to properly record and organize information, learning to prepare and present information, engaging in problem-solving with other professional staff, establishing and cultivating professional relationships, and identifying and applying ethical practices in the work place.

A primary purpose of this book is to help students effectively enhance these and other professional skills. Rather than instruct students on how this should be done, the authors present an approach that requires students to self-explore and self-analyze their decision-making process as would-be professionals in the justice system. To do so, the authors borrow concepts from the Counseling field that are applicable to professional and ethical decision-making in criminal justice and criminology.

Dr. Patricio Jaramillo, one of the authors of this book, and whose professional expertise is in counseling, believes that the major assumption behind counseling [intervention] is that through intervention individuals can learn to live effective lives, becoming effective in making better choices, think more rationally, cease ineffective or harmful habits, avoid situations that can cause them harm or reinforce bad habits. The client groups might include but are not limited to counseling with paroled criminal offenders, children, adolescents, drug-dependent individuals, marriage and family counseling, and individuals who encounter a wide range of life challenges. In general, we all experience life challenges in one form or another and chances are that these challenges are likely to influence the manner in which we make decisions in our lives. These challenges may be our inability to control anger, learned biases and prejudices, intolerance, poor interpersonal skills, passive-aggressiveness, or exhibit other emotional traits or bad habits that negatively influence our daily decision-making. If we are not careful, these influences are also likely to affect our decision-making in the workplace.

A central theme of this book is that criminal justice and criminology students bring their personal perceptions regarding criminal offenders and causes of deviant behavior to their justice profession. These perceptions are based on the students' interpretation of how their social environment is (or supposed) to be structured. However, these interpretations are not necessarily based on academic training. Many of them are grounded in the student's socialization and personal experiences that they bring to the classroom. Once in the classroom, the student attempts to frame these personal views through academic subjects and materials that supports and validates them. In part, this validation process will significantly influence the student's attitude and behavior related to the manner they perceive, interact with or treat criminal justice clients placed under their authority. For example, consider the following personal experiences of a Hispanic professional and how the academic experiences influenced and validated his perception of how part of the American justice system functions.

This person was born to a monolingual Spanish-speaking immigrant working-class family who for the most part lacked a formal education. The elementary school this person attended serviced an overwhelming number of Hispanic students who came from a similar socioeconomic background. His parents did not have a working knowledge of higher education but they valued formal education and expected their children to complete all state educational requirements. Part of this individual's upbringing included agricultural employment experiences working alongside migrant field workers some of whom may have entered the country illegally. If apprehended, they not only risked losing their much-needed jobs but could also be deported. Due to financial hardships, this person's aspirations to pursue a higher education remained unfulfilled until military educational benefits made it possible. Based on his limited world experiences, aside from personal perceptions, this person initially entered the college classroom with a limited knowledge foundation. When starting college, these early personal experiences appeared completely unrelated to academic training. However, eventually certain social science courses started to offer this individual an academic framework that reconciled his limited personal experiences with the academic environment and he was able to connect these limited experiences to a broader social context. In addition to providing an academic discipline that this person would eventually pursue, those early personal experiences combined with an academic training forged a particular professional orientation. Those early agricultural work experiences would eventually influence his academic view of the justice system. While working in those fields at a young age, it was difficult to understand why immigration officials made an effort to detain poor hard-working migrant workers who were not harming or threatening anyone. These early thought-provoking experiences eventually influenced the academic interpretation of how the American justice system functioned in its relationship to its citizens, especially as it related to minorities. It seemed that those who could impose their will against the socioeconomically disadvantaged because they had the power to do so best explained the role of the justice system. It was not the academic exposure to social perspectives that influenced the preference of one social paradigm over another; it was the personal experiences that led to the social perspective that best framed those experiences. Although this person's perspective would eventually shift, those early life experiences framed a basic outlook on the function(s) of the American justice system that, to an extent, persists to date.

Similarly, all criminal justice and criminology students bring their own personal, cultural, and work experiences to the discipline. As students, it is important that they explore how these experiences influence their perception of how the justice system operates and how suspects and offenders are treated. For example, students may interpret the causes of crime to rest within the offender's own volition. In other words, offenders commit crimes because they choose to do so by seeking some form of financial or emotional benefit. Therefore, it is within their power to decide not to offend. This belief requires a completely different policy or treatment response than if the student believes that criminal behavior is the offender's response to personal experiences over which they have little if any control. Examples of these personal experiences may include the effects of poverty, physical and emotional abuse, child neglect, psychological and emotional problems, genetic predispositions to alcohol and drug addictions that may lead to criminality, upbringing by parents who lacked proper parenting skills, associating closely with individuals of flawed character, learning from others the skills to commit criminal offenses while adopting the corresponding attitudes that facilitates committing these offenses, and a host of other factors. Or the student's perspective may reflect a belief that most offenders are poor and lack socioeconomic power because the justice system tends to protect the interests of wealthy and powerful while focusing on the disadvantaged. Figure 1 visually presents these assumptions as described in the narrative.

If criminal offenders are believed to offend because they choose to do so, punishment and incapacitation are the most likely response. If criminal offenders are believed to offend for reasons outside their control treatment and rehabilitation are the most likely responses. If both are perceived as possible contributors, the most appropriate response will most likely be a combination of punishment and rehabilitation.

An offender may be viewed as a criminal who chooses to commit crimes and therefore deserves to be punished. On the other hand, they may be viewed as a victim of circumstance because they may engage in crime for reasons that are outside their control such as poverty, or mental illness and should be given opportunities to rehabilitate. And finally, since a significant number of incarcerated persons are predominantly poor, undereducated, young, and minority, offenders may be seen as victims of the justice process that appears to protect the interests of the wealthy and powerful from the poor and powerless. Therefore, offenders may be seen as victims of the justice process. The focus is more on who they are socioeconomically than the offense(s) they have committed. A detailed discussion of the causes of crime is beyond the scope of this book. For a more thorough discussion of criminological theories, there are some excellent sources the student should consider reading [CL] (e.g., Bernard, Snipes & Gerould, 2016; Hagan, 2017).

No single interpretation fully explains the operation of the American justice system and the authors do not advocate any particular view. This argument or debate lies outside the scope of this book. However, they do believe that a person's socialization experiences serves as an important filter that is used to frame personal academic training and practices associated with one's professional experiences to the extent that eventually this socialization is likely to influence their professional responsibilities. Therefore, when enrolling in the internship or practicum course students should realize that they are not entering the agency as a blank slate upon which their internship experiences

Figure 1 Perception of the Cause, Treatment and Prevention of Crime

will be inscribed. As they start working for the agency they bring with them: personal, family, cultural, socioeconomic, gender, racial/ethnic, academic, and many other experiences that are very likely to influence the way they interpret the agency's mission and its professional environment. By extending this thought a little further, we can assume that these experiences are also likely to influence their on-the-job decision-making process. In part, this book examines decision-making in the justice system. It does not instruct students how to make decisions. It is designed to provide them with precautionary measures when making work-related decisions. It focuses on avoiding pitfalls by strengthening positive ethical and professional standards.

To better focus on standards associated with decision-making, the authors frame their approach on the *counseling assumption that individuals can learn to become effective in making better choices, thinking rationally, ceasing ineffective or harmful habits, and avoiding situations that can cause them harm or reinforce bad habits*. It is within this framework that the learning and development of professional skills and professional decision-making is strongly emphasized. To build on this framework, the authors have incorporated self-reflective exercises at the conclusion of each chapter. Since on-the-job decision-making may produce negative or positive outcomes, it is important that criminology and criminal justice students self-assess their decision-making process. Doing so may increase their awareness of potential implications associated with work-related decision-making. Our hope is that as interns their decisions will yield positive consequences and that reading this book increases the chances that this happens often.

This book is separated into eight chapters. *Chapter 1* discusses the purpose of criminal justice or criminology internship courses. *Chapter 2* describes the internship course as one of a number of courses that use personal and professional experiences to teach the practical side of a discipline to its students. Since internship courses primarily rely on teaching students through actual agency work experience, they should take significant responsibility for the learning process. However, it is important that you realize that you are not alone in this process. When they enroll in this course, they enter a partnership with the professor responsible for supervising their internship, the agency employee responsible for monitoring their internship, and university personnel responsible for assisting them with their career goals. Until they enroll in this course, the partnership is dormant and therefore inactive. The fact that their enrollment in the course is what awakens and activates the partnership reveals how important students are to this process. It is their commitment to the course that will significantly affect the energy level of the partnership. The more they interact with the other participants (supervising instructor, agency supervisor(s), and the school's "career services" professional staff), the greater the benefit of the course will be to them and all involved.

Chapter 3 emphasizes the interconnectedness of criminal justice and criminology. Through a brief analysis, the authors conclude that criminal justice policy should incorporate some aspect(s) of criminology. If it fails to address the offenders' motivation, it may be a deficient policy. To elaborate on this interconnectedness, this chapter briefly describes the main components of the American justice system such as law enforcement, prosecution and courts, probation, correctional institutions, and parole. As criminal justice and criminology students, they are, by now, well acquainted with the operation of the justice system and its responsibilities. Therefore, the review provided in this chapter is a simple and condensed reminder of the different justice system components, their responsibilities and the various employment opportunities found within them.

Chapter 4 explores the relationship between their agency internship experiences and their classroom instruction. On one occasion, a student enrolled in an internship course informed an instructor of their ability to witness the classroom material in the agency internship experiences. For a brief moment the instructor had a sense of accomplishment since his teaching seemed validated by the student's experiences. However, he later began to wonder what that actually meant? Had the student searched for this connection or was the connection inadvertently discovered? This caused the professor to consider the following question: Do students take information given to them through classroom instruction and purposely seek to make the connection through their internship experience or are these connections accidentally made? Rather than leaving this to chance, this chapter also discusses the importance of students overtly searching for the connection between their agency internship experiences and their classroom instruction.

Chapter 5 centers on the importance of criminal justice professional standards and describes how these standards can be enhanced through the internship or practicum course. As part of these standards, it offers a brief discussion regarding the use of discretionary decision-making in the justice system and offers precautions regarding its use. As a continuation of *Chapter 5*, *Chapter 6* pursues further discussion of professional standards with an extension into ethical issues as they relate to criminal justice and criminology students. It discusses how standards in the justice profession have evolved and the relevance of these standards to professional behavior in the criminal justice field today.

As a further extension of professional and ethical standards discussed in Chapters 5 and 6, *Chapter 7* describes and discusses the importance of using proper criteria when making on-the-job criminal justice decisions. It includes a brief discussion regarding the use of legitimate and illegitimate criteria for decision-making in the justice system. All professions (including the justice professions) have standards. It is important to remember that when employees (intentionally or unintentionally) violate professional or ethical standards they may experience negative personal and professional consequences.

Chapter 8 concludes this book by promoting the enhancement and/or building of important work-related skills through the internship experience. These include but are not limited to improving a student's writing skills, promoting their problem-solving skills, emphasizing their ability to organize and present information, sharpening their critical thinking skills, and fostering an ability to plan and manage projects. The effectiveness of our decision-making process is improved when our proficiency surrounding these basic skills is increased. As a matter of fact, these skills are an integral part for advancing all professional standards. While some of us may believe that focusing on such basic skills is a matter of "common sense," the authors argue that "common sense" may not be as common as we believe. If it were, the American justice system would not be experiencing so many profession-related problems as indicated by almost daily media reports of questionable behavior by justice officials during performance of their duties. In addition, the fact that some of these basic skills (such as emphasizing writing skills and organizing and presenting information) are part of any criminal justice and/or criminology academic program hopefully means that the internship course may allow students to apply them to their on-the-job experiences.

To highlight the enhancement of the aforementioned skills, the authors have included two types of instruments to this book. First, self-reflection exercises are attached to the end of selected chapters that may help students better understand their role in the justice process. Second, the book includes a journal that allows the student to record their internship experiences. Entries in this journal should include (a) information related to scheduled and unscheduled agency meetings they attend and (b) their daily internship activities. The importance of maintaining a detailed record of their internship activities and experiences is emphasized. Failing to do so may result in students forgetting important information or instructions. Having to intrude on supervisors or staff for a repeat of previously given information or instructions may appear unprofessional. However, when recording information, students should be aware that justice-related agencies often collect and use sensitive client information that must be confidentially guarded. For this reason, students should discuss the contents of their journal with their agency supervisor and follow any guidance regarding the proper recording of journal notations. The discussion should also include agency expectations and guidance regarding the student's preparation for scheduled agency meetings, recording of meeting discussions, and expected appropriate behavior during meetings.

In summary, this book has four objectives. First, it offers a review of basic but important criminal justice information that relates to the internship or practicum experiences. Since criminal justice or criminology programs generally do not permit students to enroll in internship or practicum courses until they have enrolled in and successfully completed a number of criminal justice or criminology courses, this review briefly reminds students of basic criminal justice and criminology materials to which they may have already been exposed. Second, it emphasizes the importance of decision-making in criminal justice professions. Third, it assists the students' learning process throughout the internship course from its beginning to the end. And finally, it reinforces or builds a number of basic practical skills. *It is important to remember that while the teaching and learning experience of an internship or practicum course may not be structured as a typical academic course that does not mean that the course lacks structure. An important purpose of this book is to provide this structure.*

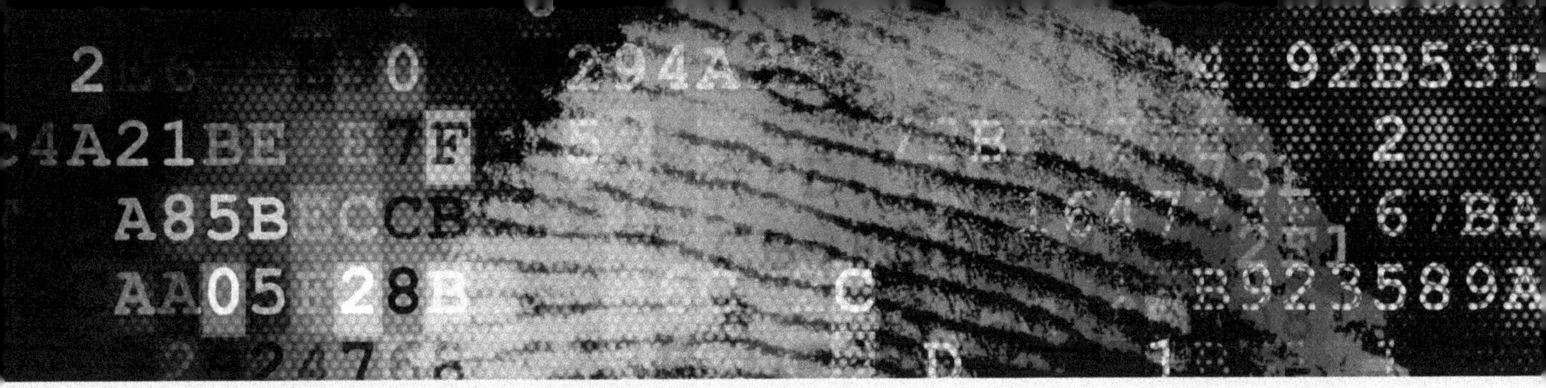

The Purpose of the Criminal Justice and Criminology Internship Experience

1

By the time students decide to enroll in an internship or practicum course, they have probably already successfully completed a number of criminal justice or criminology courses. This is important. It is inadvisable to enroll in this course before having a basic understanding of the justice system, criminal offenders, and crime victims. This general understanding of the structure and process of the American justice system and criminology is best provided through typical college courses. These academic courses can establish the necessary foundation upon which to build practical internship experiences. Building this foundation can be accomplished by (1) enrolling in courses that describe and analyze the different components of the American justice system; (2) courses that describe and critically analyze important justice-related issues and topics (i.e., race and justice, gender and justice, poverty and justice); (3) courses that critically analyze the causes of criminal behavior; and (4) courses that critically analyze crime victims and their victimization experiences. As the internship course progresses, students should explore the relationship between their criminal justice or criminology internship experiences and information they learned in criminal justice and criminology courses. It is the authors' hope that this book facilitates this process. However, before starting this search, it is important for students to understand the purposes of an internship or practicum course.

To begin, students should take a moment to reflect on why they believe enrolling in this course is important. Other than it fitting a course schedule or not having to attend a *regular* class, what benefits do students anticipate from this course? Due to its nature, the authors contend that the ultimate purpose of this course is to prepare students for employment in criminal justice-related professions. However, since successful completion of this course does not necessarily guarantee employment opportunities, this may not necessarily be its sole purpose. Our inability to identify a sole purpose for this course reflects its complexity. It is much easier to identify its structure and requirements than its purpose.

For example, the following internship course description from an established and accredited university may not identify the courses' purpose but it clearly describes its requirements.

> The student must acquire a minimum of 160 hours of practical experience in an approved criminal justice or social service agency. Unless an exception is made, the course is to be taken

> between the junior and senior years offering the student an opportunity to apply academic training in practical situations. (St. Mary's University, 2016 course catalog)

This description illustrates three baseline requirements for the course. First, before starting the internship, the placement should be approved by university officials. Second, students are allowed to enroll in the course only after successfully completing a number of other courses. And finally, students must complete a minimum number of work hours at the agency. Because of the direct nature of this course description, other than exposure to practical experiences, it is difficult to identify specific course benefits. To better gauge its value, we need to consider the course beyond its description and view it within a broader context.

Students are likely to minimally benefit from this course if they approach it from a time-fulfillment requirement (completing a number of work hours at an agency). This simply means that the student has elected to enroll in the course for the sole purpose of receiving a number of course credit hours. In this case, they show up for agency internship work until a predetermined required number of work hours are fulfilled. As long as their work quality meets the *minimum* satisfactory performance requirements, they will most likely earn a passing grade for the course. Doing this is not necessarily wrong. However, the authors propose that purchasing an education should be similar to purchasing other products. In these situations, people normally want the best product for their money. However, in reality, simply attempting to meet the minimum requirements of any college course is very likely to diminish its benefits. By doing this, students ultimately alter the quality of their education. Because of their flexibility, the authors believe that this may especially affect internship or practicum courses.

To increase the benefits of the internship experience, students should move beyond the *time fulfillmen*t requirements and find ways to glean more from the course. At a minimum, students should bring an intellectual curiosity to the course and the sponsoring agency. Wanting to learn is a key component to actually learning. Just by bringing this intellectual inquisitiveness in combination with some basic justice-related knowledge is likely to increase the value of the internship experience. While these may be two important components of the learning process, in reality, we are only describing the importance of having a general knowledge of the discipline and the need to have an inquisitive mind. The real strength of these two components actually surfaces when students add specific learning objectives to them. For example, the authors recommend that students enrolled in this course integrate the following learning objectives into their internship experience. First, compare and contrast what they have learned about formal organizations and administration with their internship experience. Second, learn to apply time management skills to professional real-world situations. Third, compare and contrast how writing styles differ between agency and academic work. Is writing for the agency supervisor similar to writing for college professors? If no, how do they differ? Why do they differ? Fourth, apply critical thinking skills to criminal justice agency problems and issues. How do these differ from their application to the classroom setting? Fifth, focus on oral communication skills. How do these differ from their application to university classes? Sixth, focus on applying problem-solving techniques in a professional setting. Again, consider how these differ from that of problem-solving requirements in the classroom? Finally, establish the goal of sharpening your listening skills. Good listening skills are critical for understanding the inner working of any professional organization. These skills and abilities coupled with the ability to properly interact with agency colleagues and supervisors can help you prepare for a successful career in the justice or related field. While the internship experience may be a rewarding one, as can be seen, to a considerable extent, it is the student who determines its true value. However, students have a number of resources available to them and therefore are not alone in this process. These include university or college administrators, professors who teach in the criminal justice/criminology department, the professor who supervises the internship course, and the agency internship supervisor (and related personnel).

Since the quality of the internship course is significantly contingent on the students' commitment to the course, it is important to discuss this *commitment* a little closer. The answer to the question of *why* a student enrolls in this course is important to this discussion. The authors believe that the student's answer to this question is found in one of two approaches. These can be described as *exclusionary* or *inclusionary* and are depicted in Figure 1.1. In the *exclusionary approach*, students make a conscious decision to enroll in the course for the sole purpose of receiving credit hours. This approach intentionally excludes or minimizes the roles of university administrators, faculty supervisors, and other instructors within the department from participating in the course process. In doing so, students decide to accomplish the minimum requirements of the course for the sole purpose of receiving a passing grade. As previously stated, there is nothing wrong with this approach. As consumers, students have the right to do this. However, the authors' preference is that students choose the *inclusionary approach*. This approach encourages students to use the available resources mentioned earlier that are intended to increase the likelihood that the internship will be a more enriching experience. However, it is important to understand that selecting this approach does not necessarily guarantee maximizing the course experience. It also requires the student's commitment and willingness to exert a greater effort to integrate available resources into the course. Hopefully, this book will help them do so.

Figure 1.1 depicts the relationship between the student and the supporting sources. In the exclusionary relationships shown by unidirectional arrows, information flows primarily from the student to the agency and academic internship supervisors. The student cultivates these relationships sufficiently to meet the requirements of each supervisor and therefore receive the necessary course credit hours. For this reason, most of the information flows from the student to the agency and faculty supervisors assuring that all basic course requirements are met.

On the other hand, the bidirectional arrows depict a different and more complicated relationship. The inclusionary approach is designed to maximize the benefits of the internship experience

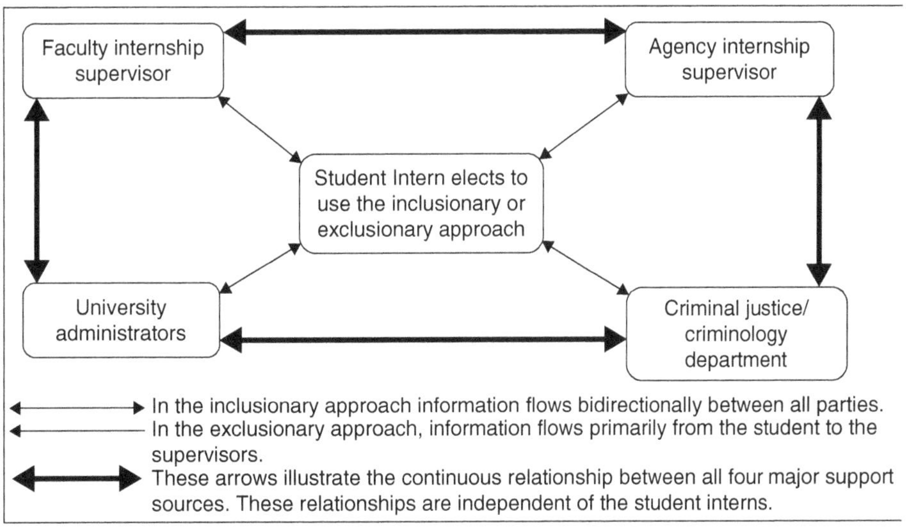

Figure 1.1 Integrating Academic Training and Professional Experiences in Criminal Justice and Criminology

by integrating information from the supporting sources into the course. Since the student ultimately decides whether to use the inclusionary or exclusionary approach, they are also in the position to influence the depth and intensity of inclusion. The thick darkened arrows show the continuous relationship between the faculty internship supervisor, the agency internship supervisor, the university or college administration and the criminal justice or criminology department. The student should include all supporting officials into the course by routinely interacting with them and keeping them informed of course-related plans and activities. Since the faculty supervisor is the primary facilitator in the process, the student should seek their guidance when planning this inclusionary approach. Below is a brief description of the relationship between the student and supporting officials.

One of the most important but often unnoticed benefits of this course will be the opportunity to work independent of direct supervision from the instructor. In the classroom, professors guide students through routine class lectures, assigned class readings, examinations, quizzes, and a variety of other course activities. However, the internship course removes this direct supervision. This may create a false impression that if the instructor is "out of sight", they should also be placed "out of mind." If students are not careful, this impression may become detrimental to their learning process. Therefore, the authors advise students to guard against this. The independent nature of the course should increase the students' effort to routinely communicate with the instructor responsible for supervising the internship. Although interning students are in a sense employed (whether paid or unpaid) by the sponsoring agency, they are still directly responsible to the university or college. The university or college is concerned about student safety when they are working at the agency and wants to ensure that the agency gives them an opportunity to maximize their learning experience. For this reason, the authors recommend that there be routine and effective communication between the student and the instructor. As part of this process, students should be familiar with the course syllabus requirements.

Students are reminded that the independent nature of internship and practicum courses creates unique challenges for instructors directing them. For example, while their interaction with students enrolled in the course is somewhat limited, these instructors are nonetheless responsible for determining if students satisfactorily complete the requirements of the course. With more than one student often enrolled in the course, the instructor must routinely communicate with various agencies that are guided by different organizational missions, goals and objectives, and often function under different work cultures. This requires instructors to interact with different agency supervisors who possess a variety of management styles. Within this context, faculty supervisors attempt to individualize learning objectives for each student enrolled in the course. Through interaction with instructors, students can help reduce the impact of these challenges. To facilitate this, the following *guidelines* are recommended. By this time, students have most likely completed some of these guidelines. They are nonetheless listed as a reminder of how all communications between students and officials are important. While reviewing them, students are reminded that communicating effectively with all parties involved in the internship course process is important.

- To begin, an initial meeting is scheduled between the student and the internship instructor. Ideally, this meeting is held before students begin their internship. This meeting should introduce students to the course and its requirements, explore the students' professional interests, and discuss how these interests can be served through the internship experience. As part of this meeting, students may select the agency with which they would like to intern.
- Once the instructor approves the agency students select, contacting the appropriate agency officials should soon follow. This serves to introduce the agency to the internship course and you

as the student applicant to them. Sometime after this introduction, during which the instructor will share all necessary information regarding the course with the agency official, you should contact the agency official(s) and initiate the application process. *This experience should be similar to the real-world employment application process.* When necessary, use your contact resources mentioned earlier to prepare for your application. During this application process, the necessary contacts among you, the instructor and agency officials should take place.

- Once students begin their internship, the instructor will periodically contact the agency supervisor to discuss your progress and make any necessary adjustments. If possible, your instructor may arrange on-site agency visits.
- Students should be familiar with the course syllabus and routinely meet with the instructor throughout the duration of the internship to discuss progress and issues of interest.
- During meetings, students should share with the instructor their written entries in the planner/organizer provided in this book. Keeping a detailed written record of internship experiences is an important part of the course. This information will eventually be used for a variety of purposes. This can be especially useful when summarizing the internship course at the end of the semester.

As students draw their internship experiences together, it may be difficult for them to understand exactly how these experiences are connected to what they have learned in the classroom. In his discussion of experiential learning, Gentry (1990, p. 9) cites George Santayana's belief that "The great difficulty of education is to get experience out of ideas." If this is true, then a key challenge to an internship course is the student's capability to integrate ideas and insights they learned in classrooms into their internship experiences. In general, it is unlikely that the students will maximize this integration process without assistance. For this reason, conferring with officials involved in the internship course may prove helpful. This is not a group of individuals coming together to explain how this integration of ideas and practice is done. However, they are available when students have questions or issues regarding their internship experiences. It is important for students to realize that they are not alone in this process.

As previously stated, students should explore the connections between the information they learned in the criminal justice and criminology courses and their internship experiences. For example, students should ask the instructor to explain or describe how they are expected to integrate these two learning experiences. When possible this conversation should also include questions regarding how the internship learning objectives fit into this integration. This discussion is especially important considering that the course instructor is responsible for supervising and eventually evaluating the internship results. As their internship progresses, students are encouraged to continuously seek their instructor's advice on how to further advance this integration. As students attempt to do this, they should simultaneously be aware of professional behaviors that officials expect from them. These include but are not limited to:

a) Wearing proper attire while working at the agency;
b) Avoiding arriving late to work or leaving work early without properly notifying supervisors;
c) Preparing for scheduled meetings;
d) Keeping scheduled appointments;
e) Turning off unnecessary electronic mobile devices during meetings;
f) Being familiar with applicable organizational rules;
g) Maintaining proper notes gleaned from meetings;

h) Avoiding unnecessary use of telephones and other electronic devices during work;
i) Avoiding unnecessary and excessive conversation during work time.

A constant awareness for behaving professionally may lead students to further develop and sharpen their professional skills and encourage them to adopt positive work habits. Their professionalism is most likely to enhance when students concentrate on solving work-related problems, properly manage time, emphasize accomplishing work deadlines, maintain proper office records, consistently document important information, efficiently and effectively manage office projects, possess good writing skills, develop and improve effective oral communication skills, improve work organizational skills, and sharpen their interpersonal skills. Developing or improving these standards should start with the initial contacts with agency officials and should continue through their entire internship. If students encounter work-related concerns during their internship, it is important that students discuss them as soon as possible with their instructor. If professors are unavailable, students should then discuss the issue(s) with an appropriate university or college administrator.

Since the internship instructor officially connects the student to the college or university, it is important to keep the instructor informed of the internship progress and related issues when they occur. Since this is not a traditional course, to a significant extent, the agency official who supervises the daily internship activities becomes the principal course instructor(s). In this role, they teach through both their professional behavior and oral/written instructions. Therefore, the student's routine communication with their academic instructor regarding the internship experiences is very important. This communication allows the instructor to be actively involved in the course process.

In earlier discussions, the authors described the importance for students to establish internship learning objectives in coordination with their academic instructor. However, the significance of these objectives extends beyond the student/instructor relationship. To the extent possible, the agency internship supervisor(s) should be apprised of these objectives. This may help them establish performance expectations for student interns and possibly assist them in identifying the work performance to be evaluated and the method of evaluation. The sharing of this information with agency supervisors will contribute directly to the students' professional development. Hopefully, agency supervisors can routinely reinforce professional standards and expectations by providing students with feedback regarding their performance. If they do not, students may request their feedback. If this is not possible, agency supervisors will upon completion of the internship finalize the evaluation process. At this time, students should receive a written evaluation of their performance. However, the authors prefer that the student receive or request periodic feedback regarding their work performance. This may allow the opportunity to correct any noted deficiencies before the final evaluation is conducted.

Students may also benefit from other university and college officials. For example, university or college staff employed by "Career" or "Professional Development Centers" or equivalent offices may help students explore potential careers. They may help students prepare their resumes, assist them in polishing their interview skills, and arrange on-campus interviews with prospective employers. This can be a valuable resource for students searching for internship opportunities or wanting work experience through volunteer connections (Penn, 2003). Service learning programs can yield positive results for all involved (Hirschinger-Blank and Markowitz, 2006). When the opportunity arises, students should discuss with their instructor the possibility of using the internship to form a partnership between them, the instructor and the university or college career services personnel. This partnership may result in two major benefits. First, it may create a broader support for the internship experience. In doing so, students will receive advice and guidance from persons other than the instructor. There is always a richness of information when it comes from a variety of sources. Second, the university or college may be able to gather important information related to internship courses and may eventually analyze this information in a manner that enhances the effectiveness of the course for future students.

Until now, the authors have discussed the role of specific officials involved in the internship process. However, since the student is the central figure in this course, a more detailed section is dedicated to them. Therefore, we are reminded that the degree of success for this course principally lies with the students' commitment to it. In this regard, the definition of "success" is placed in a broader context. For example, if students elect to use the *exclusionary approach* discussed earlier, success primarily means that the student earns a "passing" grade in the course. However, for those who elect to use the *inclusionary approach*, the definition of success extends beyond earning a passing grade. Although we know that in these cases *success* is accomplished beyond earning a passing grade, the ability to objectively measure success is not possible. Without the students' committed participation in initiating, organizing, participating, and completing this internship course, much of what is proposed in this book will be of little use. For guidelines outlined in this book to work, it is important for students to want to augment their learning of criminal justice and criminology through field practice and experience.

A typical belief holds that professional experiences for students begin after they graduate from an accredited university or college and they are hired by a criminal justice agency. If they wish, students may follow this path. However, the intersection between a students' classroom instruction and their field experience may occur sooner. For example, professors at times integrate their own professional experiences into their class assignments, invite professionals to be guest speakers in their classes, or take students on field trips to various justice agencies. However, it is the access to criminal justice and criminology internship or practicum courses that allows a more complete experience.

When the two roles of student and practitioner are compared, it seems that students seek recognition for their academic accomplishments, in turn criminal justice practitioners seek recognition through their professional commitment and skills. The latter earn professional respect and recognition through dedicated work, ethical behavior, problem-solving abilities, and strong leadership. These professional roles demand that work responsibilities and obligations are properly performed. The internship or practicum courses not only allow students to observe these qualities in action in the workplace, they are also expected to learn and display them. Students should therefore remember that as interns working in a professional agency, they represent themselves, their university or college, the criminal justice/criminology department, and their fellow students. Responsible professional behavior will reflect well on all. Unfortunately, the opposite is also true.

Therefore, students should begin to glean information from all internship or practicum experiences. They should strive to demonstrate a professional attitude and corresponding behaviors from the time they begin the internship process until its completion. It is never too early to begin developing and cultivating appropriate professional behaviors. Opportunities especially arise in the following encounters:

- As students meet with academic advisors, professors, and/or university or college administrators to discuss various parts of the internship such as exploring professional interests, discussing the requirements of the course, considering agencies that could potentially sponsor the internship, considering the effects of the internship commitment on personal and family responsibilities and work/academic schedules and how this might affect their academic performance and standing.

- Selecting a sponsoring agency and interacting with university officials as they initiate preliminary contacts with agency representatives.
- The students' interaction with agency officials as they are interviewed for the internship position.
- Being prepared in case their application is rejected and alternatives are considered.
- Reaching an agreement with agency officials regarding internship responsibilities and work schedule(s).
- Sharing, interpreting, and understanding the guidelines for evaluating the students' work performance by both the agency and academic supervisor(s).

Detailed information regarding these activities is provided in the following chapters.

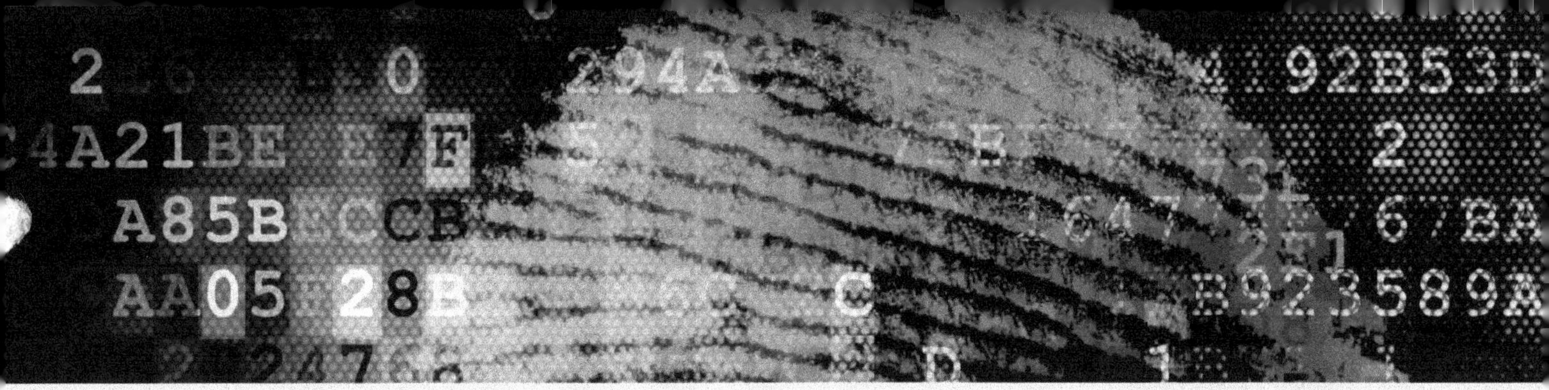

The Interaction between the Student Intern, the Academic Program, and the Agency

2

An internship course can be one of a number of experiential learning tools available to students. Sgroi and Ryniker (2002, p. 188) note that these learning tools "may range from role playing in the classroom setting, to hands-on laboratory experiences, to student-run radio stations and newspapers, to service learning in the community." Sage (as cited in Sgroi & Ryniker, 2002, p. 188) states that "experiential learning refers to learning activities that engage the learner directly in the phenomena being studied." This seems to summarize the intent of an internship or practicum course. Especially, "experiential learning is by its very nature, a form of active learning in which the student takes significant responsibility in the learning process."

In practice, the internship is an active learning process based on a four-way partnership that places significant learning responsibilities on student interns. The structure of this partnership is depicted in Figure 2.1. However, as is normally the case, the process provided by a partnership is more important than its structure. This means that the number and types of partners are subject to change. But whether the number of partners increases or decreases the role of the students should always remain central and the learning process should be consistent.

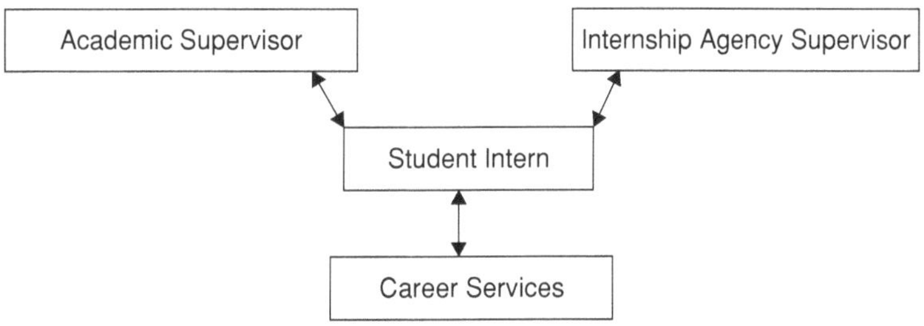

Figure 2.1 The Internship as a Partnership

Notes: Although the student intern is the center of the internship process and is supported by the Academic Supervisor, Internship Agency Supervisor and the University Administration, it is the student who should actively keep this partnership active throughout the duration of the course. The student must regularly seek the counsel and guidance from the other partners. In doing so, they are able to learn important information from them.

As the consumer (purchasing information through education) and centerpiece to this partnership, the students' commitment to the course is what fuels and energizes the process. This does not mean that other partners lack interest. Their multiple responsibilities usually pull them in different directions and are therefore unable to dedicate too much time to the needs of a few students. However, students are very likely to elicit a positive response and increased interest from these officials by displaying a strong commitment to the course. University and college professors are, in general, gratified to hear students openly express their wish to learn. It helps validate what they do. However, this observable expression will most likely energize everyone's commitment to the partnership. In reality, all but the students involved in this process serve as teachers in one way or another. The authors cannot overemphasize the significance of the students' enthusiasm in this process. So when can the student initiate this energy? The opportunity to interject their commitment to this process may start in their early contacts with school officials. This includes all initial discussions with academic supervisor(s) regarding the initial interest in the course. The expressed interest may continue as these initial discussions lead academic advisors to explain and facilitate the enrollment process and possibly share a course syllabus with the student. The syllabus is likely to explain the goals and expectations of the course. As the semester progresses, the academic advisor may also periodically meet with the student and, if permitted, with the agency supervisor. In doing so, the agency supervisor also has opportunities to share their goals and expectations with the student and the academic supervisor. Finally, the university administrators responsible for promoting the students' professional development may provide the student with assistance regarding the preparation of resumes, teaching interview skills, and career planning. This structure and communication process establishes a foundation that supports the student's active learning process. A key objective of the partnership is to help students explore the meaning of "active learning" and help them apply this concept to their internship experience. By applying the idea of active learning throughout their various internship experiences, students can continuously energize the learning process.

Student interns rely primarily on experiential learning—rather than lectures, reading assignments, or typical examinations. It is, therefore, difficult for professors to share with students a select knowledge base. Close examination of a typical course syllabus will usually uncover required or recommended textbooks that students are expected to read. In support of these reading assignments, professors will organize and deliver lectures that support the reading assignments and eventually administer a series of examinations to evaluate how well students retained portions of this shared knowledge base. Sometimes professors will give students writing assignments hoping to interject a critical thinking component into their teaching. If internship or practicum courses do not include these requirements, how do the students identify and acquire a necessary knowledge base?

Again, attention is directed to the student's role in the learning process. However, before doing so we are reminded that the absence of these typical course requirements may give the erroneous impression that internship and practicum courses do not have a knowledge base and therefore lack structure. This is not necessarily true. The difference is that in typical classroom courses instructors organize their syllabi around a series of learning objectives. They identify a plan of action (from beginning to the end) to be followed throughout the duration of the course and will most likely outline a detailed knowledge base. In turn, internship course syllabi are most likely to identify how to initiate the internship and the necessary procedures to successfully end the course. But since the nature of these courses is founded on learning through experience, the knowledge base will be either nonexistent or unclear. The most plausible person to identify and construct this knowledge base is the internship student. This book provides the tools to do so.

The student builds this knowledge base by doing three things. First, before starting their work at the agency, students should reflect on the criminal justice and criminology courses they have completed to date. As part of this reflection, they should glean materials from these courses that relate to the agency they have selected. Second, based on these gleaned materials, students should identify and write objectives they wish to learn from their soon-to-be agency experiences. This is important because it draws a connection between their already acquired classroom instruction and their future agency experiences. Third, they should document as many of their internship experiences as they are able to. To make this record keeping easier for the student, the authors have included a journal and a planner in this book. Because of our many obligations and daily busy schedules, we often forget more information than our memory retains. A purpose of this journal and planner is to help minimize this "information overload" that often results in our forgetting important information. For expediency, we often try to commit information to memory because taking time to write something down seems to take too long. However, as we all know by now, we soon tend to forget such things. Without consistently documenting their internship activities, students will most likely forget important details. The authors therefore recommend that as part of their internship students develop the habit of maintaining a detailed written record of their internship experiences and related observations.

How many times have we had a calendar-planner only to find out that either we do not use them or we use them improperly? The most common reasons or excuses for not using them are because "we believe the situation does not warrant its use," "we're in a hurry," "takes too much time write the information and we're sure we can remember it." Or, when we use one, to save time, we write the information "cryptically" by writing fragmented statements. Unfortunately, when we review the information it may appear unclear. Maximizing the use of a planner takes discipline and time. To use it appropriately, students should develop the discipline of routinely using the planner and when using it, they should write the necessary details. Students should therefore consider the journal/planner as a professional tool. As with any tool, it is only as useful as students make it. To facilitate this process a blank journal is attached to the end of this chapter.

The journal is divided into three sections. The first section asks that students record the goals and expectations of all persons involved in the internship process. This includes the student, the internship academic supervisor, the agency supervisor, and those of other university or college administrators who may be involved in the process. In the second section, students are asked to record information regarding all scheduled agency meetings that they are asked to attend. However, it is advisable that they give the agency supervisor an opportunity to review the written notes before sharing them with anyone and consider the supervisor's instructions. The third section asks that students maintain a daily journal of their internship activities and observations while working at the agency. Again, they should give their agency supervisor the opportunity to review their notes before sharing them with anyone else. Here too, they should consider the supervisor's instructions.

To increase the quality of information to be recorded in this journal, students might want to discuss the use of the journal with the academic and agency supervisors. This may be especially useful if they can help incorporate the student's internship goals and expectations when recording their internship experiences. Through separate meetings with their academic supervisor, agency supervisor, and the university's career development officials, students may ask them to voice their own expectations. Students may schedule brief meetings (which should not exceed 20 minutes) with each one. To expedite the process, students should share with them the topic(s) to be discussed before the meetings take place. However, before doing so, students should be prepared to discuss their own goals and expectations. This will give students the opportunity to initiate the process with their own expectations already identified.

Any "experientially" based course should require the recording of agency experiences as a part of the learning process. We therefore recommend that these experiences be documented and their content analyzed and categorized at the completion of the course. The journal serves a dual purpose. As an agenda planner, it can help the student manage the work time more efficiently and maintain a clearly written record of relevant experiences. Although keeping brief incomplete notes that have particular meaning only to the student may be expedient, this practice should be avoided. Trying to decipher important information from cryptic notes at a later time may be challenging and result in potential problems ranging from simple embarrassment to the loss of professional confidence by agency administrators.

Student interns should commit to perform employment duties in a professional manner for an agency at the direction of an agency supervisor(s). This becomes their primary source of learning for this course. *We understand that while the teaching and learning experience may not be structured as a typical academic course, it does not mean that the course lacks structure. As a matter of fact, this book attempts to provide a significant portion of this structure.* An important purpose of a criminal justice or criminology internship course is to prepare the student for future employment in the justice professions. Common to all these professions is the art of decision-making—decisions that often have a direct impact on people's lives. This justice system decision-making process starts from the point where a police officer decides to stop and search a suspect, to someone deciding to impose the death penalty for a convicted offender. All students who decide to enter a justice profession must be prepared to eventually make on-the-job decisions. In part, this book focuses on professional decision-making. Learning to make well-informed decisions is less likely to result in problems for employees who make them and administrators who supervise them. Figure 2.2 describes real-life examples of, to say the least, questionable decision-making by justice officials and related consequences of those decisions.

Justice Officials	Summary Description Incidents
Incident regarding *police* decision-making.	A Haitian immigrant was arrested by police and taken to a police station and allegedly sodomized with a broken broomstick. The man was awarded a monetary settlement and police officers were sentenced to prison terms.
Incident regarding *prosecutorial* decision-making.	A former prosecutor was disbarred for allegedly committing a number of ethics violations during his involvement in an investigation of three college athletes accused of rape, kidnapping, and sexual offenses.
Incident regarding a *state attorney general's* decision-making.	The Kansas Supreme court suspended a former state attorney's right to practice law in that state for allegedly violating "Kansas Rules of Professional Conduct" while serving in that position.
Incident regarding a *judge's* decision-making.	A state judge was given a prison sentence and ordered to pay restitution for allegedly sentencing juvenile offenders to maximum prison sentences. He allegedly received bribes and kickbacks from private prison officials who could profit from these extended offender stays.
Incident regarding a *probation officer's* decision-making.	A county probation officer reportedly faced felony charges for allegedly soliciting sex in exchange for handling certain features of an offender's case such as supervision fees and jail detention.
Incidents regarding *corrections officials'* decision-making.	A corrections officer employed by a major state prison system allegedly accepted an inmate's challenge to a fight and then staged an assault by the inmate to justify his injuries. Facing felony charges, the officer pled no contest to reduced charges.
Incidents regarding *parole officers'* decision-making.	Soon after a judge sentenced a former parole officer to prison for allegedly accepting bribes from a client, four other officers were facing similar charges.

Figure 2.2 Examples of Unethical Decision-Making by Justice Officials

While Figure 2.2 describes incidents alleging official misconduct, it does not identify the cause(s) for this behavior. Regardless of the reasons, these behaviors are inexcusable and they came with consequences. Like all professions, the criminal justice profession has standards and as one experienced criminal justice professional said—"when officials violate these standards they do so at their own peril."

Learning to make proper professional decisions cannot come too early. Criminal justice ethics taught in a typical college classroom is a good start. However, witnessing actual daily decision-making in a criminal justice agency offers a robust learning experience. Given the opportunity, student interns should take advantage of observing and analyzing professional decision-making as part of their internship experiences. This allows them to explore and learn more about the criminal justice profession they eventually wish to enter. It is important to note that while making appropriate routine profession-related decisions may enhance their careers, making "bad" decisions can compromise those same careers. Above all, students should seek and cultivate professional attitudes and behaviors through their internship experiences.

Self-Reflection Assignment One: Identifying Professional Internship Goals and Expectations

Planning and starting an internship is similar to planning and initiating a trip. The two most important things to know when taking a trip are one's destination and directions how to get there. While the unexpected experiences are usually the most interesting part of a trip, not knowing one's destination, direction and planned activities along the way are likely to result in some bad experiences. Similar to taking a trip, students should know when and where their internship starts and when it will end. And yes, the unanticipated experiences will be some of the most interesting learning experiences of the internship course. However, as the internship unfolds students must guide its direction by accomplishing a series of preplanned activities. These preplanned activities are based on predetermined learning goals and objectives. To begin this process, once the agency approves the student's application to intern with them, students should schedule an interview (not to exceed 20 minutes) with the professor who will be supervising and grading their internship. Students should use the questions provided below to guide the interview and write responses in the provided spaces. Second, students should repeat this process with the person(s) who will be supervising their internship at the agency.

Interview with the *internship academic supervisor*:

Question 1: Can you describe the major learning goals that I should strive for while interning at the agency? Write the answer in the space provided below.
Your response:

Question 2: Can you describe specific objectives or methods that I as a student can use to accomplish these major learning goals through my agency experiences? Write the answer in the space provided below.
Your response:

Interview with *internship agency supervisor*:

Question 1: Can you describe the major learning goals that I should strive for while interning at the agency? Write the answer in the space provided below.
Your response:
Question 2: Can you describe specific objectives or methods that I as a student can use to accomplish these major learning goals through my agency experiences? Write the answer in the space provided below.
Your response:

Self-Reflection Assignment Two: Maintaining Detailed Agency Meeting Notes

All agencies expect their employees to behave professionally. This especially applies to attending scheduled meetings in a timely fashion and to be attentive during these meetings. Student interns are not exempted from these expectations. However, before attending any meeting, it is important for students to first confirm that their presence in the meeting is requested or welcomed. Assuming their presence is required or welcomed is not a good idea. The confirmation will avoid awkward and embarrassing situations. If their attendance is welcomed, students should avoid unprofessional behaviors while the meeting is in progress. This sometimes occurs unintentionally. For example, the unnecessary use of portable electronic devices during the meeting may make students appear distracted—a behavior others may see as offensive. Inclusively, it is often best to listen more than speaking when participating in meetings. Normally, if administrators have a question or want an opinion, they will ask. When this happens, due to their busy schedules, administrators do not usually expect detailed explanations or discourses. This may be a basic difference between agency work and a college environment. In their search for answers professors normally ask students to elaborate on issues since detailed answers demonstrate understanding. This is part of the college or university learning process. However, agency administrators are usually searching for an answer to a work-related issue or problem. Administrators seek information that often helps them resolve a problem. Therefore, when students are asked to express an opinion or viewpoint during meetings, we suggest they answer the question as directly as possible. If officials wish for more information, they will pursue the matter. At the conclusion of the meeting, officials expect students to be better informed. It is therefore important to listen and write all relevant information during the meeting. Students should not rely on their memory to later remember details regarding guidance and instructions given during meetings. It does not professionally reflect well if students have to go back to administrators and employees for basic information disseminated during meetings. However, it is acceptable to later ask for clarification as the issue(s) or problem(s) is/are addressed. For this reason, we strongly recommend that students use the following planner to record what they consider "important" or "relevant" information pertaining to these meetings. If officials distribute a meeting agenda before the meeting, we advise that students familiarize themselves as much as possible with topics to be discussed at the meeting. In summary, students should confirm their presence is welcomed at the meeting; during the meeting, they should be attentive and ask relevant questions; they should use the planner to write what they consider important information pertaining to meeting (e.g., instructions given); and if necessary, they should ask follow-up questions or clarifications any time after the meeting. They should always remember that they have only one professional reputation that should not be compromised.

Date of Meeting	Attended (yes or no)	Topics Discussed or Reason for not Attending
Date of Meeting	Attended (yes or no)	Topics Discussed or Reason for not Attending
Date of Meeting	Attended (yes or no)	Topics Discussed or Reason for Attending

Date of Meeting	Attended (yes or no)	Topics Discussed or Reason for not Attending
Date of Meeting	Attended (yes or no)	Topics Discussed or Reason for not Attending
Date of Meeting	Attended (yes or no)	Topics Discussed or Reason for not Attending
Date of Meeting	Attended (yes or no)	Topics Discussed or Reason for not Attending
Date of Meeting	Attended (yes or no)	Topics Discussed or Reason for not Attending
Date of Meeting	Attended (yes or no)	Topics Discussed or Reason for not Attending
Date of Meeting	Attended (yes or no)	Topics Discussed or Reason for not Attending
Date of Meeting	Attended (yes or no)	Topics Discussed or Reason for not Attending
Date of Meeting	Attended (yes or no)	Topics Discussed or Reason for not Attending
Date of Meeting	Attended (yes or no)	Topics Discussed or Reason for not Attending
Date of Meeting	Attended (yes or no)	Topics Discussed or Reason for not Attending
Date of Meeting	Attended (yes or no)	Topics Discussed or Reason for not Attending

Date of Meeting	Attended (yes or no)	Topics Discussed or Reason for not Attending
Date of Meeting	Attended (yes or no)	Topics Discussed or Reason for not Attending
Date of Meeting	Attended (yes or no)	Topics Discussed or Reason for not Attending

Date of Meeting	Attended (yes or no)	Topics Discussed or Reason for not Attending
Date of Meeting	Attended (yes or no)	Topics Discussed or Reason for not Attending
Date of Meeting	Attended (yes or no)	Topics Discussed or Reason for not Attending

Self-Reflection Assignment Three: Documenting Internship Activities

An important part of justice agency practices is the gathering, processing, and use of information. While a variety of agency information sources may exist, an important and often overlooked source is information gleaned by a person's participation in agency activities. It is this type of information that significantly impacts our effectiveness as criminal justice professionals. The activity journal provided on the next page is a good starting point for students to begin this information gathering process. This daily documentation of agency participation allows them to analyze what they do on a daily basis and helps them assess the progress of activities over time as these activities unfold. The number of agency work hours required by the internship course is somewhat limited when compared to the amount of experience made available by the agencies. In other words, there is much to learn in such a limited time. For this reason, students should maximize their experiences by documenting them in this daily journal. Upon completion of the internship, a review of the written experiences may surprise students by their expanse. In other words, they learned more than they realized. While engaged in the course, students should remember to stay focused and record the details of their internship experiences.

Date (Month/Day/Year)	Entry 1: In the space below, write all activities performed for the agency while on duty on this date. Include number of hours worked.
Date (Month/Day/Year)	Entry 2: In the space below, write all activities performed for the agency while on duty on this date. Include number of hours worked.
Date (Month/Day/Year)	Entry 3: In the space below, write all activities performed for the agency while on duty on this date. Include number of hours worked.

Date (Month/Day/Year)	Entry 4: In the space below, write all activities performed for the agency while on duty on this date. Include number of hours worked.
Date (Month/Day/Year)	**Entry 5: In the space below, write all activities performed for the agency while on duty on this date. Include number of hours worked.**
Date (Month/Day/Year)	**Entry 6: In the space below, write all activities performed for the agency while on duty on this date. Include number of hours worked.**
Date (Month/Day/Year)	**Entry 7: In the space below, write all activities performed for the agency while on duty on this date. Include number of hours worked.**
Date (Month/Day/Year)	**Entry 8: In the space below, write all activities performed for the agency while on duty on this date. Include number of hours worked.**
Date (Month/Day/Year)	**Entry 9: In the space below, write all activities performed for the agency while on duty on this date. Include number of hours worked.**

Date (Month/Day/Year)	Entry 10: In the space below, write all activities performed for the agency while on duty on this date. Include number of hours worked.
Date (Month/Day/Year)	Entry 11: In the space below, write all activities performed for the agency while on duty on this date. Include number of hours workeded.
Date (Month/Day/Year)	Entry 12: In the space below, write all activities performed for the agency while on duty on this date. Include number of hours worked.
Date (Month/Day/Year)	Entry 13: In the space below, write all activities performed for the agency while on duty on this date. Include number of hours worked.
Date (Month/Day/Year)	Entry 14: In the space below, write all activities performed for the agency while on duty on this date. Include number of hours worked.
Date (Month/Day/Year)	Entry 15: In the space below, write all activities performed for the agency while on duty on this date. Include number of hours worked.

Date (Month/Day/Year)	Entry 16: In the space below, write all activities performed for the agency while on duty on this date. Include number of hours worked.
Date (Month/Day/Year)	Entry 17: In the space below, write all activities performed for the agency while on duty on this date. Include numbers of hours worked.
Date (Month/Day/Year)	Entry 18: In the space below, write all activities performed for the agency while on duty on this date. Include number of hours worked.
Date (Month/Day/Year)	Entry 19: In the space below, write all activities performed for the agency while on duty on this date. Include number of hours worked.
Date (Month/Day/Year)	Entry 20: In the space below, write all activities performed for the agency while on duty on this date. Include number of hours worked.
Date (Month/Day/Year)	Entry 21: In the space below, write all activities performed for the agency while on duty on this date. Include number of hours worked.

Date (Month/Day/Year)	Entry 22: In the space below, write all activities performed for the agency while on duty on this date. Include number of hours worked.
Date (Month/Day/Year)	Entry 23: In the space below, write all activities performed for the agency while on duty on this date. Include number of hours worked.
Date (Month/Day/Year)	Entry 24: In the space below, write all activities performed for the agency while on duty on this date. Include number of hours worked.
Date (Month/Day/Year)	Entry 25: In the space below, write all activities performed for the agency while on duty on this date. Include number of hours worked.
Date (Month/Day/Year)	Entry 26: In the space below, write all activities performed for the agency while on duty on this date. Include number of hours worked.

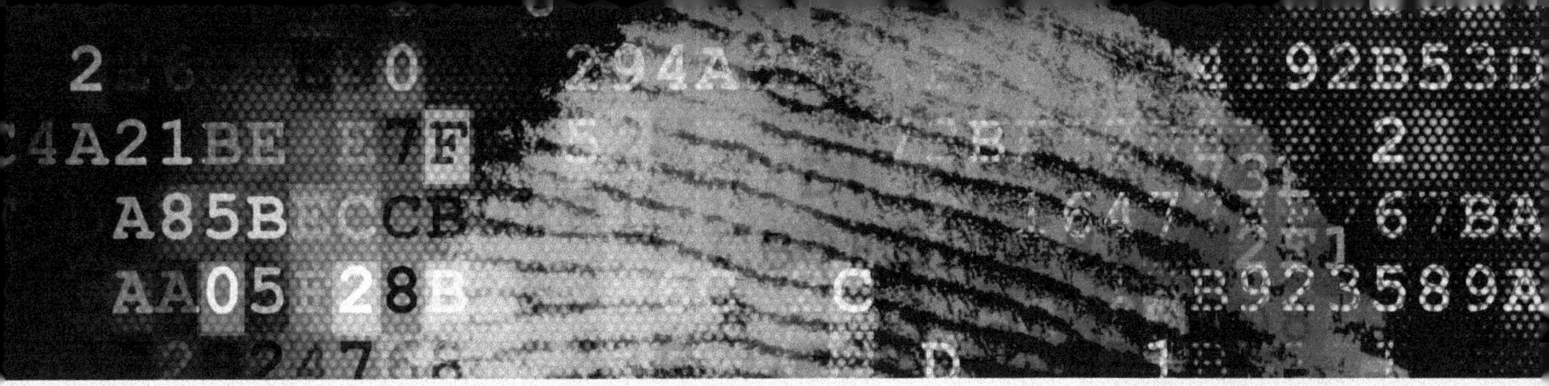

Training and Education for the Criminal Justice Profession

3

Students interested in *criminal justice* or *criminology* are sometimes unable to clearly distinguish between the two disciplines. This initial confusion is often due to the overlapping materials between the two. Similar to a coin, the two sides can be distinguished but they are inseparable. To begin, we propose that *criminal justice* is the study of the role of formal organizations such as police, courts and prosecution, probation, prisons, and parole that have been established to assist the prevention and control of crime. In turn, *criminology* focuses on the study of the causes, treatment, and prevention of crime. Of the two disciplines, criminology has existed longer. For example, Karmen (as cited in Hancock and Sharp, 2000) points out that the current criminal justice system was nonexistent during the American colonial period. It was the American Revolutionary War and writing of the Constitution that initiated changes that eventually led to the modern American justice system. It therefore appears that social and political forces operating at the time influenced the origins of the American justice system revealing that it did not develop in a socio-political vacuum. Just as external forces influenced its early development, they too continue to significantly influence changes in the justice system today. Students of criminal justice and criminology should therefore stay informed of current social, political, and economic forces that might further influence important changes in the system. A good practice would be to review laws or legislative bills adopted during state and federal legislative sessions. This examination might reveal potential or real impacts to the justice system.

Historically, the study of criminal justice has to a significant extent coincided with developments in the study of criminology. For example, a major founder of the classical school of criminology, Cesare Beccaria (which attributed the cause of crime to an offender's "free will"), also recommended major changes to the justice system intended to compliment the new theory of the cause of criminal behavior. Although the idea of criminology came first, a focus on the criminal justice system as a separate area of study eventually surfaced. As a precursor to these programs, August Vollmer, the first police chief of Berkley, California, helped establish the first criminal justice program at the University of California, Berkley in the early 1900s (Prout, 1972). The program focused on professionalizing policing and reducing corruption in law enforcement. However, it was the Law Enforcement Assistance Administration (LEAA) responding in part to the social conflict and perceived racial injustices of the 1960s that was responsible for the rapid expansion of the discipline. This social conflict was characterized by various forms of disorder including clashing social values, city riots, and rampant crime. Since police were, for the most part, the initial responders to these situations, some scholars believe that at times unfair blame was attributed to police for a number of these problems. (Samaha, 2006).

Compared to criminal justice, *criminology* tends to primarily focus on the causes, prevention, and treatment of criminal behavior. This includes the study of individual and social ecological factors that are associated with crime in society. As earlier stated, criminology is the older of these two disciplines. Since the study of criminal behavior is the study of human behavior, tracing the evolution of criminological theories to its roots is not easily done. For example, Bernard, Snipes and Gerould (2016, p. 3) state that "… Hippocrates (420 B.C.) provided a physiological explanation of thinking by arguing that the brain is the organ of the mind." This makes it very difficult to date the beginning of the formal study of Criminology. However, it was Cesare Lombroso, a 19th-century medical doctor who is credited with applying the scientific method to study criminal behavior for the first time. It therefore seems that the first positivist theory of criminal behavior was biological (Bernard, Snipes and Gerould, 2016). Since then, a variety of psychological, sociological, and bio-social theories of criminal behavior have developed, evolved, and are still evolving. A number of these theories have become central to the study of the causes of criminal behavior. We can therefore conclude that similar to criminal justice, criminology is also an interdisciplinary science.

For justice policy purposes, the disciplines of criminology and criminal justice are like the two sides of the same coin. Each side may be distinct from each other but they are nonetheless inseparable. Criminology explores factors that influence people to commit crimes and criminal justice explores how best to detect, adjudicate, and control criminal offenders. In reality, it is somewhat difficult to develop, implement, or study modern criminal justice policy without giving some serious consideration to the role of the cause(s) of criminal behavior. For example, if we believe that offenders engage in criminal behavior based solely on their "free will" for the purpose of satisfying a personal need or want requires a different criminal justice policy response than if we believe that offenders commit criminal acts due to reasons outside their control. These reasons could include but are not limited to poverty, psychological problems, personality disorders, peer pressure, socialization, and/or biological factors. Crime control policies that are based on the premise that offenders commit crimes because of free will are likely to include "deterrence" as a central goal. The belief is that if a person commits a crime because they want to, then the policy goal should be *to make them not want* to commit the crime. Therefore, harsh punishment for deterrence purposes is the criminal justice system's most likely response. However, if the justice policy is based on the belief that offenders commit crimes due to forces outside their control, then the justice system is likely to target the elimination or neutralization of these forces. If so, the policy may include a "rehabilitative" component to its response. A key problem with not knowing the causes of criminal behavior is that an incorrect assumption will most likely result in wasted financial, social, and political capital.

What sets criminal justice apart from other professions is the unsolicited intrusion of criminal justice professionals into people's lives. For example, parents voluntarily bring their children to schoolteachers. Patients voluntarily visit medical doctors, psychologists, therapists, or counselors. Parishioners not only voluntarily attend places of worship they also offer financial support and services to their rabbis, priests, or pastors. However, police, prosecutors, judges, probation officers, corrections officials, and parole officers usually intrude uninvited into the lives of citizens. For this reason, the courts have found it necessary to regulate this intrusion in attempts to balance the rights of individual citizens with the right of the government (e.g., criminal justice system) to intrude in their lives. As we know by now, the system is imperfect. However, with all its imperfections, the system has proven to be functional. A brief summary description of each criminal justice system component is discussed below. These include policing, prosecution, judicial proceedings, probation, correctional institutions, and parole.

Policing holds a special place in the justice process. Aside from serving as the entrance to the justice system, it provides the most direct contact with the public. While it is difficult to assess the quality of this relationship (some segments of the public see it as positive while others are likely to disagree with this opinion), in general, police and communities share a mutual respect and have learned to depend and work with each other. In an analysis of *police* and communities, Kelling (as cited in Hancock and Sharp, 2000, p.147) explains that "the quiet revolution is beginning to make itself heard: citizens and police are joining together to defend communities." He seems to refer to the creation of community policing and problem solving policing strategies. Community-oriented policing is "a police strategy primarily concerned with establishing a working relationship with the community" and problem-oriented policing is a "police strategy that is primarily concerned with identifying, analyzing, responding to, and assessing community problems related to crime and neighborhood quality of life" (Samaha, 2006, p. 199). Although these two strategies differ from each other, they both tend to work as police community partnerships. The adoption of these strategies has expanded the police relationship and responsibilities with their corresponding communities. Their goals have been transformed from primarily focusing on crime control efforts to that of controlling crime, reducing the public's fear of crime, maintaining public order, and improving neighborhood living conditions (Samaha, 2006). It is difficult for this transformation to occur without the police giving some consideration to better understanding why people commit crimes. For example, Uchida (as cited in Hancock and Sharp, 2000) points to improved effective decision making by creative police organizations who did so by merging their policy development with social science research techniques.

In the face of this trend, we can anticipate with a strong level of certainty that the relationship between police and communities will continue to significantly influence policing strategies in the future.

Albonetti states that "the decision to charge is the most discretionary decision (meaning it's the least subject to review) in all of criminal justice" (as cited in Samaha, 2006, p. 298). The official responsible for filing criminal charges against a defendant is the *prosecutor*. Because of its powerful impact on the lives of accused offenders and crime victims, McCoy (as cited in Samaha, 2006) considers the prosecutorial process as one of the most important steps in the justice system.

The police bring cases directly to the prosecutor whose further investigation of the case can lead to a number of dispositions. One of these is the decision to bring the case to court for a formal trial. Since they must now prosecute the case, the prosecutor's power directly connects police to the courts. And if court procedures determine defendants to be guilty of criminal charges, the prosecutor may now have direct input on the sentencing process. This involvement may also influence the connection between court procedures and the corrections process. This prosecutor's influence on the system is best summarized by Samaha (2006, p. 283) who states that "prosecutors are a vital link between police, and courts and between courts and corrections." It is within their power to adjust the prosecutorial process to address the needs of individual offenders ranging from failing to prosecute a case to requesting that the judge consider a specific punishment or related options. Among their many responsibilities, prosecutors are perceived as "tailoring the law to suit individual defendants' needs" (Samaha, 2006, p. 285). To make these determinations, the prosecutor may consider the socio-psychological needs of the offender and the danger or risk that offenders present to the community. In doing so, the prosecutor may give serious consideration to the motivations of the offender. If the prosecutor wishes to pursue a stricter sentence such as incarceration they may seek to formally indict the offender.

After the official indictment is issued, the *offender, judge, defense attorney, and prosecutor* may either reach a plea agreement or formally adjudicate the case in court. If the offender eventually pleads guilty to the criminal charge(s) or a judge/jury determines the offender to be guilty beyond a reasonable doubt, the offender will then be sentenced.

Before sentencing the offender, the *judge may instruct the probation department* (in some jurisdictions this may be mandated by law) to conduct a pre-sentence investigation and submit a written report of the findings to the court. Through this investigation, the probation department determines the level of risk the offender presents to the community and its analysis of social, emotional, psychological, alcohol and/or drug dependency, and other personal issues helps identify factors that may have influenced the offender's decision to commit the crime. Based on the pre-sentence investigation recommendations, the court may sentence the offender to *probation*. In addition, the court may impose specific conditions on the probationer. These may require that the offender seek counseling, attend alcoholics' anonymous meetings, and/or demand complete abstinence from alcohol. Some scholars separate these conditions into distinct categories depending on their purpose. For example, while some conditions may be considered routine and are imposed on all probationers others may be intended to be more punitive or rehabilitative (Samaha, 2006). If probationers violate probation conditions or commit additional crimes, they may have their probation revoked and may be sent to a correctional institution where they can serve the remainder of the sentence.

If the court determines that the offender presents a significant risk of reoffending or if the crime is so serious that a probated sentence is unacceptable, *incarceration* may be the next sentencing option. If so, the offender serves the sentence in a correctional institution instead of serving it in the community. All offenders arriving to prison will be temporarily assigned to a *classification* process where they will undergo a series of interviews and testing to determine security risks they present to the institution and identify any special needs they might have. Based on this information, inmates are routinely given a security level classification and assigned to a particular correctional institution. When they arrive at their assigned institution, based on classification criteria, the inmates are then assigned to appropriate housing areas and given the freedoms and restrictions dictated by their classification level.

Depending on applicable laws, inmates may be eligible to be conditionally released from prison before they complete their incarceration sentence. The process for releasing an inmate on parole is not completely dissimilar to the process of placing an offender on probation. A hearing is conducted where parole officials consider the inmates' institutional adjustment and other factors associated with the offender's criminal history. Usually, one of three basic outcomes may result from the parole board hearing. First, parole officials may determine that the offender's risk of reoffending is too high. In this case, the parole request can be denied and the person may be required to serve the remainder of their sentence in prison. Second, the offender may be denied parole release and another hearing is scheduled sometime in the future when the offender's progress can be reevaluated and the granting of parole reconsidered. Or, the offender may be granted parole and allowed to serve the remainder of the sentence in the community. Similar to probation, if the inmate is granted parole, release conditions may be attached to the parolees' supervision (Samaha, 2006). Any conditions placed on the offender by parole authorities are normally enforced by a supervising *parole officer* who is assigned to monitor the offender while in the community. As with probation, "if parolees violate any of these conditions," to "if parolees violate these conditions," they may be sent back to prison where they might serve the remainder of the sentence. In general, offender rehabilitation goals are part of the *probation, prisons, and parole* services. To effectively do so, the offenders' motivation for criminal behavior is given serious consideration.

In summary, criminal justice and criminology can be considered two distinct academic disciplines. However, their application to the justice process results in a significant overlap. Police officials, prosecutors, defense attorneys, judges, probation officials, prison officials, and parole officials in one form or another consider why offenders commit crimes when deciding how to process the accused. For this reason, preparing university students for the justice professions should include training and instruction in both criminal justice and criminology.

The immediate response by police and fire fighters to the September 11, 2001, terrorist attacks in New York serves as an example of how much our communities depend on the assistance of their local justice officials. The subsequent controversial issues regarding our constitutional standards related to the investigation, prevention, interrogation, prosecution, pre-hearing detention, and punishment of suspected terrorists are a further testament to the growing complex relationship between American citizens and the justice system. Years later, some of these issues are still pending in American courts awaiting judicial solutions, while other challenges are likely to surface in the future. This is the proverbial tip of the iceberg and further exploration of these issues is outside the scope of this book. For our purpose, it is sufficient to realize that the increasing complex relationship between justice officials and the community is creating new challenges for criminal justice and criminology academic programs whose purpose is to train future justice professionals. It is this relationship that typically brings up important questions and issues regarding the effective training of criminal justice and criminology students.

As previously asserted, with the exception of internship courses, most criminal justice and criminology courses are primarily taught through traditional classroom pedagogical methods. In comparison, the internship course primarily requires students to complete a certain amount of work hours in an approved criminal justice or social service agency. These situations limit the role of the instructor to directing the student from a distance or perhaps periodically meeting with them when the need arises. For the student, their agency internship supervisor becomes the principal instructor. It is this unique course structure that raises the following questions regarding its teaching effectiveness. Is the purpose and value of internship or practicum courses simply to offer practical experience for the student? What is the student expected to learn? How are these learning objectives structured? How is the student expected to demonstrate knowledge of these objectives? To answer these and other related questions, the internship course needs to be structured within a framework that incorporates an active and structured participation between all persons involved in the internship process. The remaining chapters are dedicated to forging this framework, clarifying these relationships, and reinforcing their interaction.

To increase the course benefits, students should closely examine their internship role within the agency. Once they start, the learning process in this course is likely to take an unfamiliar direction. Normally, students will not be required to meet regularly with their academic instructor, attend lectures or take examinations as they usually do in other courses. But this does not detract from the value of the course. It is a different course structure that simply requires a different approach. This book attempts to delineate a blueprint for this approach. However, much of this courses' success depends on the students' awareness that the internship experiences are likely to strengthen their knowledge of criminal justice and criminology in ways that traditional courses are unable to do so. To place this chapter in perspective, students should complete the attached self-reflection exercise. However, they should first examine Figure 3.1 and then follow the instructions in the reflection exercise.

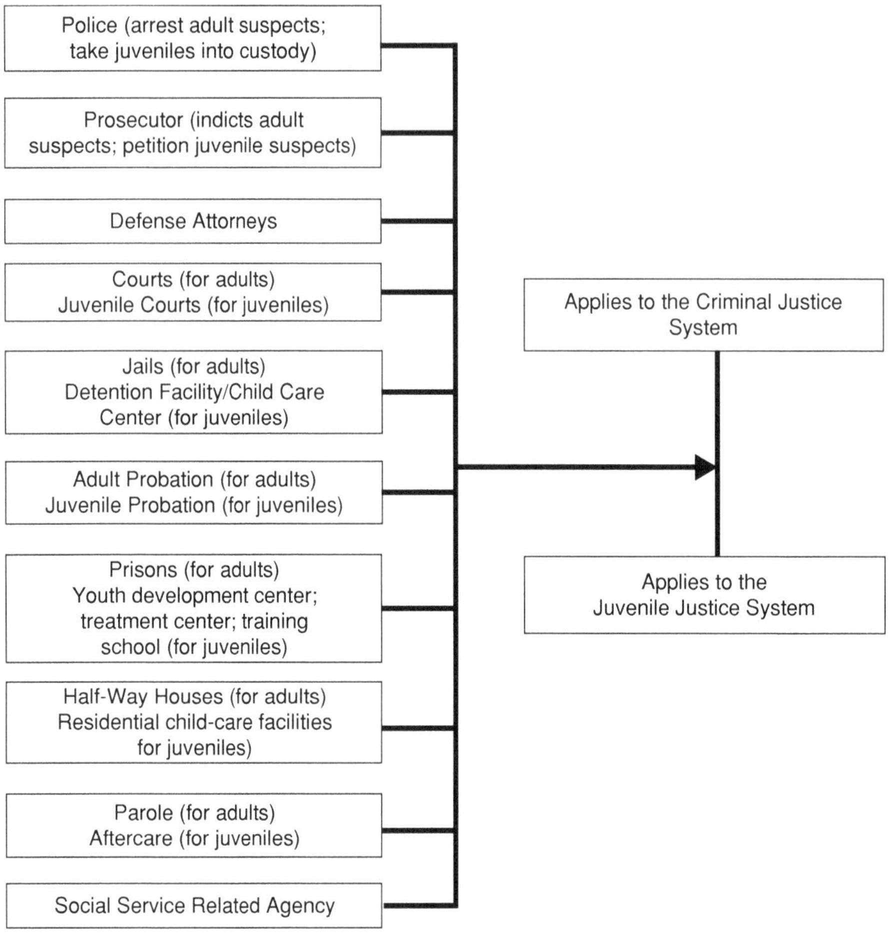

Figure 3.1 Components of the Criminal and Juvenile Justice Systems

Notes: This figure lists major components of the American adult and juvenile justice systems. However, the true complexity of the system lies in its discretionary decision-making and interdependency of the components.

Self-Reflection Assignment Four: Contemplation of the Professional Field

The justice professions include a broad variety of public and private criminal justice and related fields. Not surprisingly, it employs professionals from criminal justice, criminology, sociology, political science, psychology, and other related disciplines. It seems that regardless of one's academic discipline, there appears to be employment possibilities in the justice field. This variety may create somewhat of a challenge for criminal justice and criminology students when searching for and selecting an agency to sponsor their internship. Since this can directly impact your career interests and choices, it is important that you seriously consider this challenge. To help you in this process, a brief listing of agencies that may offer employment opportunities is provided in the figure below. To complete this assignment, please review the various professions listed in this figure and select the agency from which this profession is most likely to derive from. Once you've selected the agency, answer the following questions.

What is your academic major? (Check only one)

☐ Criminology ☐ Criminal Justice ☐ Other: ______________________________

A	B	C	D	E	F	G	H	I	J
Police (arrest adult suspects; take juveniles into custody)	Prosecutor (indicts adult suspects; petition juvenile suspects, victim services)	Defense Attorneys	Courts (for adults) Juvenile Courts (for juveniles	Jails (for adults) Detention Facility/ Child Care Center (for juveniles)	Adult Probation (for adults) Juvenile Probation (for juveniles)	Prisons (for adults) Youth development center; treatment center; training school (for juveniles)	Half-Way Houses (for adults) Residential child-care facilities for juveniles)	Parole (for adults) Aftercare (for juveniles)	Social Service Related Agency (e.g. child protective services, A.G. child protective services)

1. From the above-listed professional areas, identify the area from which your internship derives:

   ____

2. Based on your knowledge of the justice system, in the space provided below describe and discuss what you believe this profession's mission should be:

3. In the space provided below, describe how this professional area is related to your academic discipline:

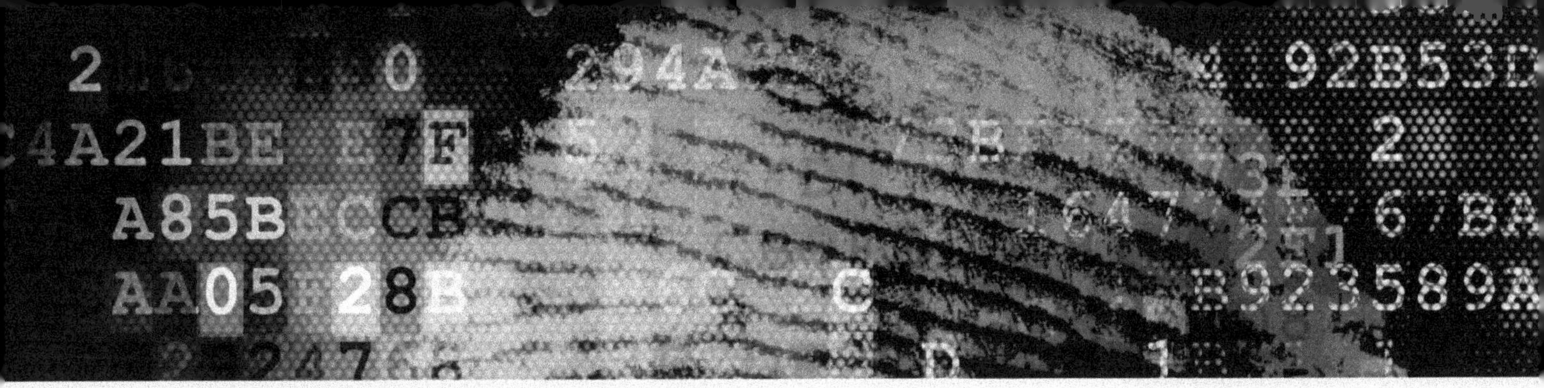

Connecting the Agency Internship Experiences with the Classroom

4

The previous chapter briefly described the structure and process of the American justice system and highlighted decision-making responsibilities as one of its most critical elements. In turn, this chapter will address the development and sharpening of skills that when combined with effective decision-making is likely to enhance the interns' overall professionalism. However, before discussing these skills, it is important to appraise how the agency internship experiences are connected to the student's classroom instruction. Students who isolate their internship experiences from what they have learned in their previous traditional courses and fail to appreciate the potential contributions the course may have on their future professional development are cutting off the course from the past and future. Doing this is likely to undermine the internship course effectiveness. Stone and McLaren (1999, p. 171) surmise that "internships and experiential learning have always been a controversial subject among educators." Why would this be controversial? Could it be that a student is enrolled in a course where the instructor relies on someone else to primarily direct the course? Could it be that instructors cannot identify objective criteria that can be used to evaluate the students' performance? Could it be that instructors are unable to objectively prove that the student has learned something of value? Could it be that instructors are unsure about the agency's commitment to do what's best for the student? Could it be that instructors are concerned that students are being used for "busy work," such as filing documents rather than engaged in activities that truly expose them to learning something important?

Debating the benefits of experiential courses is likely to continue unabated. However, for now, we should try to identify and increase their benefits and eliminate as many negative effects associated with their disadvantages as we can. For example, some scholars believe that internships help students identify and solidify their professional interests. Others believe that students will be more satisfied with their initial employment opportunities by performing and learning to value "work-related" outcomes (Stone & McLaren, 1999). In addition, Hall (as cited in Stone and McLaren, 1999, p. 172) notes that

> interns are also expected to make an easier transition from school to the criminal justice workplace because they do not experience the shock when they find that the work environment is not what their academic preparation or the media have led them to believe.

By making this point, Hall indirectly identifies a number of issues. For example, there is a gap between the way the media projects the criminal justice system and the realities of criminal justice professions. This has always been well understood by the criminal justice profession. The distinction between the media goal of entertaining the public and our mission to protect the public and provide justice for the accused and guilty offenders should be discussed in typical criminal justice and criminology courses. However, it could be argued that the internship experience will prevent or lessen the "shock" for students when they as Hall writes "find that the work environment is not what their academic preparation led them to believe," it would be (as cited in Stone & McLaren, p. 172). This needs further discussion.

If through their internship experiences, students discover that their academic preparation failed to teach them the realities of the justice system, we can assume that the quality of the academic program needs to be addressed. Especially, the primary purpose of any criminal justice program is to discredit criminal justice and criminology myths and teach the realities of the system and factors associated with criminal behavior. In this regard, the internship experience gives the student an opportunity to compare their own classroom instruction with that of the real-world criminal justice experiences. The internship experiences students describe in the attached journal and planner can be used to make this comparison. This discussion leads to the following three important questions. First, do students ignore their academic training when performing their internship duties and treat them as two separate and unrelated experiences? Second, do students put aside their academic training when performing their internship duties and treat them as two separate but slightly related experiences? And third, do students seek to validate their academic training through their internship experience? These are questions that can only be answered by the students themselves.

Ignoring Classroom Instruction when Performing Internship Duties: Gelb (1998) reminds us that much of human learning takes place through imitation. As part of their internship, students are placed in situations where they can learn by internalizing behaviors of agency practitioners. The students are now learning outside of their "normal" academic environment and the daily reinforcement of academic values is now replaced by daily "work values." The practitioner influence cannot be underestimated. For example, let us imagine that upon starting their first criminal justice job, the new employee is informed by an agency practitioner that "real" criminal justice is learned in the field rather than the classroom. Would the student accept this advice? If we believe this does not occur, we should ask ourselves, why not? How many times have we heard the saying, "those that can't do, teach." The matter of higher education may be a source of conflict between practitioners who possess it and those who do not. This becomes more apparent when they will eventually compete for intra-agency promotions. Regardless, to denigrate a persons' academic achievement is to say the least, inadvisable. However, when it does happen, this bad advice will most likely affect those students who are unable to identify a functional link between their classroom instruction and their internship experience.

Separating the Academic Training from Internship Experiences: Students may choose to intern with a selected agency out of simple convenience. For example, the agency may include operating hours on weekends or evenings and thereby offer the student a flexible work schedule that they desire. If this is the case, the student is likely to enter the agency with a few preconceived expectations. As the internship experience unfolds, the student may from time to time inadvertently detect a relationship between their classroom instruction and agency operation. However, this may not be true if the student intentionally works at integrating their acquired classroom knowledge with their agency experiences. This may be easier said than done. It is more likely that students will bifurcate their learning experiences by focusing on their internship experiences while at the agency and their academic materials while in the classroom. Occasionally, the two may overlap when the student is reminded of an academic learning experience while working at the agency or vice versa. However, students are more likely to be excluded from a complete learning experience when they do not consciously attempt to integrate the two learning experiences.

Validating Academic Training through Internship Experiences: By the time students report to their sponsoring agency, they should have researched their options and professional interests. Ideally, the starting point rests with the student's academic classroom experiences which may introduce them to agencies associated with the justice system. Whether the student already had an interest in this agency or was unsure of what agency they wanted to intern for, any previous academic training regarding this agency should have been considered and the philosophies and practices that guide the operation of the selected agency should have been explored. Validating any classroom-related instruction through the internship experience requires students to consult their course syllabi, lecture notes, and textbook materials related to the criminal justice profession in which they have chosen to intern. If the information is not readily available, the student is encouraged to obtain these materials from instructors who teach courses related to these agencies. While interning, students should continuously search for connections between classroom instruction and the internship experience. The students' ability to strengthen the connection between these two experiences maximizes their internship learning process and will enhance their knowledge of the justice profession they have selected.

Conclusion and Student Self-Reflection: This chapter describes the importance of the relationship among the criminal justice or criminology program, student interns, and the internship agency. For practical purposes, the typical classroom instruction in criminal justice or criminology can be separated from the more pragmatic internship training. However, the two share a similar goal of improving the quality of future criminal justice practitioners. Regardless of the training, eventually it is the quality of employees that determines the success of each justice-related agency. To increase the learning benefits of their internship experience, students should select an agency based on reasons other than just convenience. The selection should be based on their professional interests and while selecting, they should learn as much as possible about the agency and its corresponding criminal justice branch (police, courts and prosecution, community corrections and institutional corrections). While working for the agency, the student should consistently search the relevancy of their criminal justice and criminology academic training. To do so, the students should (1) review course syllabi, lecture notes, and textbook materials from courses they completed and that are related to the agency for which they plan to intern; (2) they should confer with instructors whose courses they completed that are related to the agency where they intend to intern; and (3) they should be prepared to apply some of these materials to the agency training they will eventually receive.

Self-Reflection Assignment Five: Process for Selecting the Internship Experience

While conversing with a former prison official, a law enforcement officer wondered out loud how the prison official had been able to work in what he believed to be a challenging environment. In response, the former prison official also acknowledged the unique challenges of law enforcement. Needless to say, it is well known that all justice-related professions have their share of serious challenges. And although these challenges may differ from each other, they are equally demanding. It is interesting to note that criminal justice and criminology students are not discouraged by these anticipated challenges as they prepare for their careers. Quite the opposite, their career interests appear to be constant. Fortunate for the justice field, students seem to have a varied interest in justice-related professions. This ensures that all criminal justice branches (law enforcement, community-based corrections, correctional institutions, juvenile justice) will have sufficient and qualified applicants. For this reason, criminal justice and criminology college professors do not normally favor a criminal justice profession over another and tend to welcome the various professional interests. These professors are primarily interested in preparing students for the career challenges that lie ahead. They understand that the successful operation of justice-related agencies depends on the quality of their employees. Although there are various criminal justice and criminology courses that help prepare the student for their future profession, the internship course serves the student in a variety of ways. One way is to help them explore career opportunities by offering them hands-on criminal justice experiences. The following exercise attempts to focus on these career interests by connecting the internship experience with the students' academic training. To conduct this reflective exercise, complete the following assignments.

Assignment 1: Considering your ***professional interests****, in the space provided below, briefly describe the reasons why you chose to intern with this agency.*
Your response:

Assignment 2: In the space provided below, list and briefly describe the ***academic courses*** *that you have successfully completed and that you believe are related to the mission and practices of this agency.*
Your response:
Assignment 3: Considering the ***academic justice related training you have received to date****, in the space provided below, describe how this directly applies to your agency internship. If it does not, explain why?*
Your response:

Assignment 4: Take the opportunity to ***discuss your responses*** *with your academic internship supervisor. This information may help the university/college make important changes to its training curriculum. In the space provided below write a brief summary of your discussion.*
Your response:

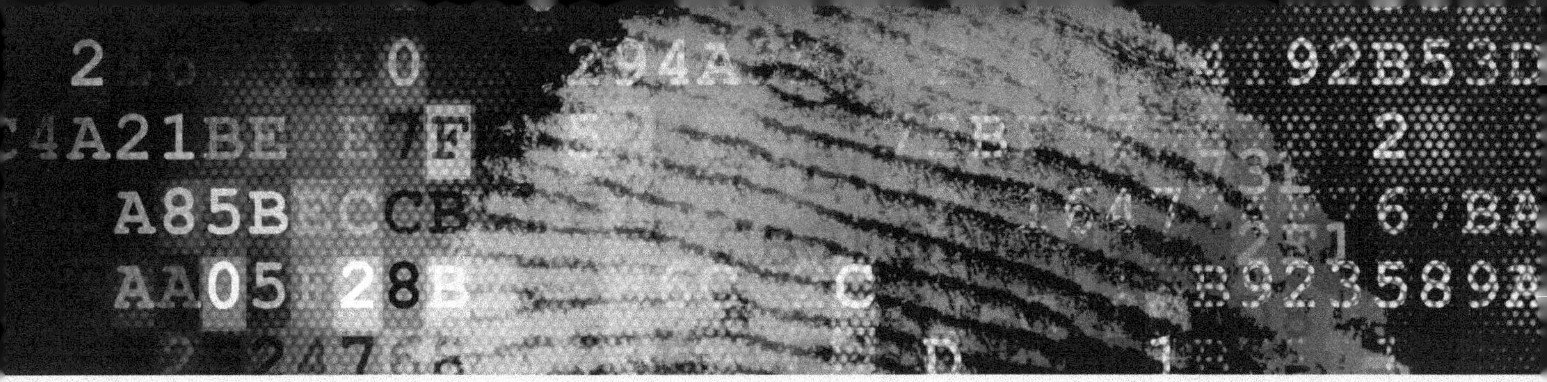

Decision-Making and Justice Profession Standards

5

The previous chapter briefly reviewed the various components of the American justice system and described their interconnectedness. Figure 5.1 visually depicts the structure of these components. However, within this structure lies a complex and demanding formal and informal decision-making process that fuels and drives the system. It is this discretionary decision-making process that transforms the practice of criminal justice and applied criminology into professions. Criminal incidents may tend to share a similar frame such as the type of law(s) violated (property or violent crime) and location(s) where they are perpetrated. However, the circumstances surrounding each crime differ. When a crime is reported or witnessed the police may arrest a suspect, if arrested, prosecutors may charge the suspect, if charged, the suspect may go to trial, if the suspect goes to trial they may be declared guilty, if declared guilty, the offender may be imprisoned or placed on probation, if placed on probation the offender's probation may later be revoked and sent to prison, if imprisoned the offender may be placed on parole, if paroled, this too may be revoked and the offender may have to serve the remainder or a portion of their sentence in prison. Whether justice officials act or refuse to act against the offender at any stage of the process depends on the circumstances surrounding the incident. Having the authority to act on one's discretion within broad parameters is an important characteristic of a profession. Occupations that require a repetitious process and do not allow the use of discretion in their decision-making process are unlikely to be considered professional positions.

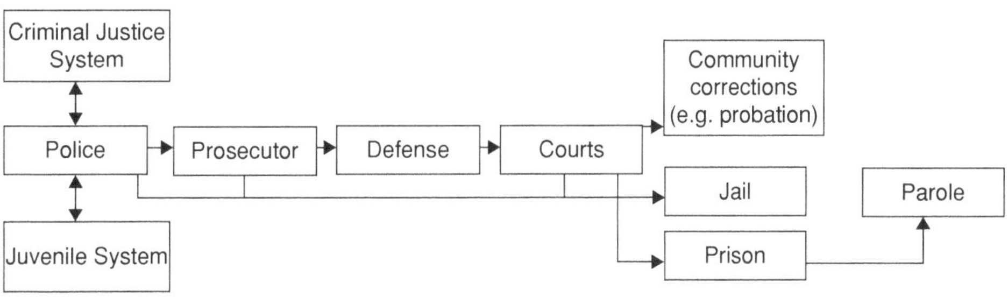

Figure 5.1 Structure and Flow of the Criminal Justice System

Samaha (2006, p. 9) notes that "like all processes, criminal justice makes 'products.'" To explain this concept, he states that

> law enforcement officers produce suspects when they arrest (or otherwise focus their investigation on) a person. Prosecutors produce defendants when they charge suspects with crimes. Courts produce offenders when they convict defendants. Corrections produce ex-offenders when they release them from custody.

As previously noted, these "products" are generated by a discretionary decision-making process used by justice officials. It is this discretionary justice that drives and transforms the system into a profession. This chapter discusses this decision-making process and delves into its impact on the criminal justice system and its clients. We present this brief analysis within the framework *that through internship and practicum courses criminal justice and criminology students can learn to become effective in making better decisions, thinking rationally, ceasing ineffective or harmful decision-making habits, and avoid decision-making patterns that can cause them harm or reinforce bad habits.*

While decisions made by police, prosecutors, judges, probation officers, and prison officials yield a criminal justice product, the variety of decisions are numerous, ranging from deciding not to act in particular situations to gradually and deeply increasing their intrusion into a person's life (Samaha, 2006). To summarily grasp the variety of decisions made by the justice system, we can contemplate and make a mental list of the responsibilities we know pertain to law enforcement, prosecution, judicial and corrections personnel. While we understand that this is only a fraction of the decisions made throughout the justice system, it nonetheless allows insights into the system's complex and demanding responsibilities.

History and the media reveal that justice officials have not always made the best decisions regarding the processing of its "product." This is not surprising when we consider the intrusive nature of the criminal justice system. This intrusive and often coercive nature of the justice system is very likely to cause conflict between justice officials and citizens. Think of the times we are driving somewhere and a police car happens to be directly behind us going in the same direction. How does that generally make us feel? The first thing that probably crosses our mind is the speed limit on that stretch of road and then we confirm that we are driving within the specified limit. Next, we hope that the car passes us or turns to a different direction soon. This somewhat uncomfortable relationship between justice officials and citizens that is best understood within the context of Supreme Court decisions related to different criminal justice branches. These decisions, whether judicial and constitutionally based either place limits or expand the authority of justice officials by dictating what they can and cannot procedurally do when interacting with the public under certain circumstances. Below is a brief discussion of selected United States Supreme Court's decisions. They are reviewed for the purpose of examining the significance of criminal justice professional standards.

The Importance of Discretionary Decision Making: The distinction between the academic fields of criminology and criminal justice and their importance to developing justice policies has already been discussed. As a brief reminder, criminal justice centers primarily on the study of the *administration and practices* of justice agencies that have been established to control crime while criminology focuses on the study of the *causes, treatment, and prevention of crime.* Despite these differences, both disciplines actively contribute to the operation of criminal justice agencies.

Putting our academic training aside, as employees of the justice system, it is important that we ensure the justice system performs judiciously and responsibly. If every person who acts suspiciously becomes a suspect and every suspect a defendant and every guilty defendant an incarcerated offender, and every incarcerated offender a parolee, the justice system would most likely collapse under its own weight. It is the ability of justice professionals to prudently use discretion during their on-the-job decision-making that prevents this from happening. However the misuse of discretion may create serious problems (Gaines and Miller, 2014). Throughout the justice process, (either formally or informally) criminal justice professionals conduct a *risk and needs assessment* when dealing with clients. For example, a police officer may decide not to arrest suspects because the officer believes that they do not present a serious threat to the community and that with some minimal intervention, the suspects may cease "their, not so serious anti-social or deviant behavior." The officers' decision may be based on the perceived degree of danger a suspect poses and the circumstances surrounding the officer/suspect contact. A prosecutor may decide not to officially charge a suspect with a crime because the suspect does not present a serious threat to the community and like the police officer the prosecutor decides that a less punitive intervention is the most appropriate response. The prosecutor's decision may be based on a belief that the suspect is unlikely to commit further offenses. This formal/informal *risk assessment* process repeats itself countless times throughout the system on a daily basis involving decisions by judges, adult and juvenile probation officers, adult and juvenile parole officers, jail officials, and prison officials. These determinations are based on two important assumptions. First, officials may assume that certain factors influence the person's behavior. For example, the person may be considered young, immature, and inexperienced and therefore tends to make bad decisions. In such situations, the formal processing of the person through the justice system may be more detrimental than helpful. The second assumption may be that the person needs assistance and guidance to help them make better decisions. Through research, criminologists have identified social and psychological attributes that correlate with crime and delinquent behavior. These may include but are not limited to neighborhood conditions, dysfunctional family relationships, socioeconomic status, peer influence, peer rejection, and/or poor academic performance. Justice officials who use this type of objective information to conduct formal and informal risk and needs assessments regarding the disposition of criminal justice clients are more likely to reach effective decisions. However, information provided in Figure 5.2 reveals that this is not always the case. As part of the academic training, we often study Supreme Court decisions as they relate to the justice system. Figure 5.2 lists and briefly describes a selected number of cases that have affected various branches of the American justice system. It is important to remember that the events that eventually resulted in each Supreme Court case decision listed in this figure started with a discretionary decision made by a criminal justice employee(s). We can only assume that the person(s) on the receiving end of that decision decided to legally challenge it because they believed it to be unfair and therefore unconstitutional. Since the Court sided with the plaintiff(s) in some instances and with the defendant(s) in others, one can conclude that the reasoning used by the justice employees in these cases was at times flawed but not in others. In turn, the Supreme Court's authority to fundamentally establish legal precedent means that when the plaintiff prevailed the justice system had to amend its practices to meet the requirements of these new laws.

When justice professionals make questionable moral and/or legal decisions, the consequences can be personally and professionally significant. However, an upside to these bad situations has been professional improvements to the operation of the justice system. Current criminal justice practices and standards have been greatly influenced by a number of U.S. Supreme Court cases. These cases usually originated with an interaction between justice officials and average citizens. These persons decided to legally challenge specific practices of justice officials and the Court decided in their favor forcing the system to change. Two things to remember from this brief discussion is that (1) anyone employed by the justice system can be a defendant in these cases and (2) that when plaintiffs prevail, these Court decisions will directly impact the administration of justice in the United States. As justice professionals we are given the privilege to make discretionary decisions when intruding in peoples' lives. However, this privilege comes with responsibilities. A review of the Supreme Court cases outlined in Figure 5.2 reminds us of the importance of these responsibilities. Therefore, our responsibility when making these decisions should not be taken lightly. All criminal justice employees (current and future) should make every effort to rid themselves of habits that compromise their rational reasoning when interacting with others. This especially applies to situations where we occupy positions of authority.

The following Supreme Court decisions are adopted from Cole and Smith (2004). The reader should refer to this text for a more detailed discussion of these important legal cases (see Figure 5.2).

Example of Supreme Court Cases that have affected the Administration of Policing

1. In the case of stopping motorists under *special circumstances*, the Supreme Court decided in "City of Indianapolis v Edmond (2000) that police traffic checkpoints cannot be justified as a generalized search for criminal evidence; they must be narrowly focused on a specific objective" (p. 218).
2. For police to *stop and frisk* a person, the Supreme Court ruled in "Adams v Williams (1972) that officers may rely on reports from reliable witnesses as a basis for conducting a stop and frisk" (p. 218).
3. In *incidents leading to arrests*, the Supreme Court ruled in "Chimel v California (1969) that to preserve evidence and protect the safety of the officer and the public after a lawful arrest, the arrestee and the immediate area around the arrestee may be searched for weapons and criminal evidence" (p. 218).
4. In *searches of open fields*, the Supreme Court ruled in "Oliver v U.S. (1984) that officers are permitted to intrude on private land that are open areas, such as fields and pastures, but they may not search the yard area immediately surrounding the house (curtilage) without a warrant or a specific justification without a search warrant" (p. 209).
5. As to the questioning of suspects, the Supreme Court ruled in "Miranda v Arizona (1966) that before suspects under police custody may be questioned, they must be told that they have the right to remain silent, that anything they say may be used against them, and that they have the right to counsel during questioning" (p. 223).

Example of Supreme Court Cases that have affected the Administration of Prosecution and Courts

1. Regarding the *rights to counsel* challenges, the U.S. Supreme Court determined in "Powell v Alabama (1932) that indigents facing the death penalty who are not capable of representing themselves must be provided with an attorney" (p. 325).
2. In *Gideon v Wainwright (1963)* the U.S. Supreme Court determined that "indigent defendants must be provided with attorneys when facing serious charges in state courts" (p. 325).
3. In *Argersinger v Hamlin (1972)* the U.S. Supreme Court decided that "indigent defendants must be provided attorneys when facing misdemeanor and petty charges that may result in incarceration" (p. 325).

Example of Supreme Court Cases that have affected the Administration of Probation and Parole

1. The U.S. Supreme Court established in *Mempa v Rahay (1967)* that "state probationers have a right to counsel at a combined revocation-sentencing hearing" (p. 445).
2. The Court later established in *Gagnon v Scarpelli (1973)* that "before probation or parole can be revoked, the offender is entitled to a preliminary and a final hearing and to specific elements of due process" (p. 444).

Example of Supreme Court Cases that have affected the Administration of Correctional Institutions

1. In the case of mail censorship, the Supreme Court decided in *Procunier v Martinez (1974)* that "censorship of mail is permitted only to the extent necessary to maintain prison security" (p. 487).
2. As to the inmate's protection from unreasonable searches and seizures, the Supreme Court determined in *Hudson v Palmer (1984)* that "officials may search cells without a warrant and seize materials found there" (p. 488).
3. Prison inmates have also challenged prison conditions claiming that they are cruel and unusual as prohibited by the Eighth Amendment to the U.S. Constitution.
4. In *Ruiz v Estelle (1980)* the U.S. Supreme Court declared that "conditions of confinement in the Texas prison system is unconstitutional" (p. 489).
5. As to the disciplining of prison inmates, the Supreme Court determined in *Wolff v McDonnell (1974)* "that the basic elements of procedural due process must be present when decisions are made concerning the disciplining of an inmate" (p. 491).

Example of Supreme Court Cases that have affected the Administration of Juvenile Justice

1. In *Kent v U.S. (1966)* the U.S. Supreme Court decided that "courts must provide the essentials of due process in transferring juveniles to the adult system" (p. 539). The following year in *In re Gault (1967)* the U.S. Supreme Court determined that "in hearings that could result in commitment to an institution, juveniles have four basic constitutional rights" (p. 539).
2. Three years later in *In re Winship (1970)*, the U.S. Supreme Court decided that "in delinquency matters, the state must prove its case beyond reasonable" (p. 539). Before this decision, proof beyond reasonable, applied only to adults.

Source Adapted from: Cole and Smith (2004).

Figure 5.2 Supreme Court Cases that have Influenced Criminal Justice Standards

In conclusion, a complete review of U.S. Supreme Court decisions regarding intrusive practices by police, courts, probation, parole, and corrections officials is outside the scope of this book. Presenting this brief review of U.S. Supreme Court decisions related to each criminal justice component serves two purposes. First, it reveals that suspects and criminal offenders often engage in social and/or physical confrontations with justice officials and that some of these confrontations are eventually litigated in court. These confrontational incidents typically result from disagreements when justice officials attempt to exercise or impose their authority.

At times, these confrontations may unexpectedly arise from seemingly innocuous situations. This could involve police officers stopping and searching someone while acting on their legal authority and the suspect believes them to be overzealous. A prosecutor may decide to charge someone with a crime and the citizen believes the prosecutor to be vindictive. A judge may decide to punish someone and people believe the sentence to be excessive or too lenient. A jail official may decide to administratively segregate an inmate and the inmate feels that the reclassification is unfair and unjustifiably restrictive. A prison director may decide to ban certain publications from entering a prison system and inmates may feel that such a ban is unwarranted and therefore unconstitutional. Or, a parole official may decide to intensify the supervision of a parolee and the parolee interprets this action is unnecessarily intrusive. Therefore, when possible and time permits, caution should be taken when reaching on-the-job decisions.

Supreme Court decisions contribute to criminal justice professional standards by giving justice administrators clear legal decisions regarding official actions that are either permitted or prohibited under given situations. Regardless of their outcome, these cases remind criminal justice and criminology students that their on-the-job criminal justice-related decision(s) could for one reason or another come under legal scrutiny. Litigation emanating from these confrontations may result in both criminal and civil liabilities for the defendant. Therefore, it is imperative that students learn to make decisions based on objective and prudent reasoning. When possible, it is advisable to follow agency approved and established policy and practice. We should remember that the ability to act under the authority of any criminal justice profession carries serious responsibilities. The authors reiterate their hope that *through internship and practicum courses criminal justice and criminology students can learn to become effective decision makers that are able, to think rationally and exercise professional judgment while ceasing ineffective or harmful decision-making habits, and to avoid decision-making criteria that can cause them professional harm or reinforce bad habits.*

Decision-making and Criminal Justice Internship or Practicum Courses: The probability that a student enrolled in an internship or practicum course would be asked to make serious agency related decisions is probably zero. The legal liabilities for the agency would be too great. However, this does not preclude students from seeking advice and guidance from their agency internship or practicum supervisor regarding the decision making process in their profession. For example, students can learn decision-making protocols to be followed when confronted with particular problematic incidents or situations. The following self-reflection exercise is designed for this purpose.

Student Reflective Exercise Regarding Decision-Making: Academic internship supervisors welcome the students' willingness to explore and analyze their internship role in their respective agencies. A purpose of the self-reflective exercises included in this book is to help students with this self-analysis. While this chapter emphasized the importance of decision-making in the justice field, to better understand this process, students are asked to complete the following self-reflection exercises related to decision-making. Specific criteria and issues regarding decision-making in criminal justice are discussed in more detail in the next chapter.

Self-Reflection Assignment Six: Analyzing Agency Decision-Making Processes

Some people have said that it is best to make a wrong decision than to make no decision at all. While there may be some truth to this, the authors believe *that it is best to make a well-informed decision than to make no decision at all.* As justice officials, we are expected to make on-the-job decisions. While the majority of these decisions are routine and may not have a far-reaching impact on clients, the agency or the justice system, some inadvertently or intentionally do. The almost constant access to the news media makes it inescapable to read or hear of justice officials who have made unwise decisions in the performance of their professional duties and the fact that we learn about them through the news media probably means that these decisions are of the far-reaching impact variety. Since bad things are likely to happen when careless on-the-job decisions are made, it is therefore important that criminal justice and criminology students explore decision-making processes in their interning agency. These processes are often deeply ingrained in agency practices and may be difficult to fully comprehend when cursorily reviewed. It is nonetheless important that students attain some insights into the importance of making decisions in justice agencies. To do so, please complete the following assignment. First, the student should make arrangements to interview the agency internship supervisor(s). Since agency administrators are often busy, this meeting should be brief and probably not exceed 20 minutes. During this interview, students should ask the administrator the following three questions and write their responses in the form provided below.

Question 1: In your opinion, what are the five most common problems/situations confronted by you or other employees when doing their job?
Your response:

Question 2: What are the typical responses to these problems/situations?
Your response:
Question 3: Based on your professional experiences, what "protocols" should guide employee decision-making when confronted with difficult or problem situations?
Your response:

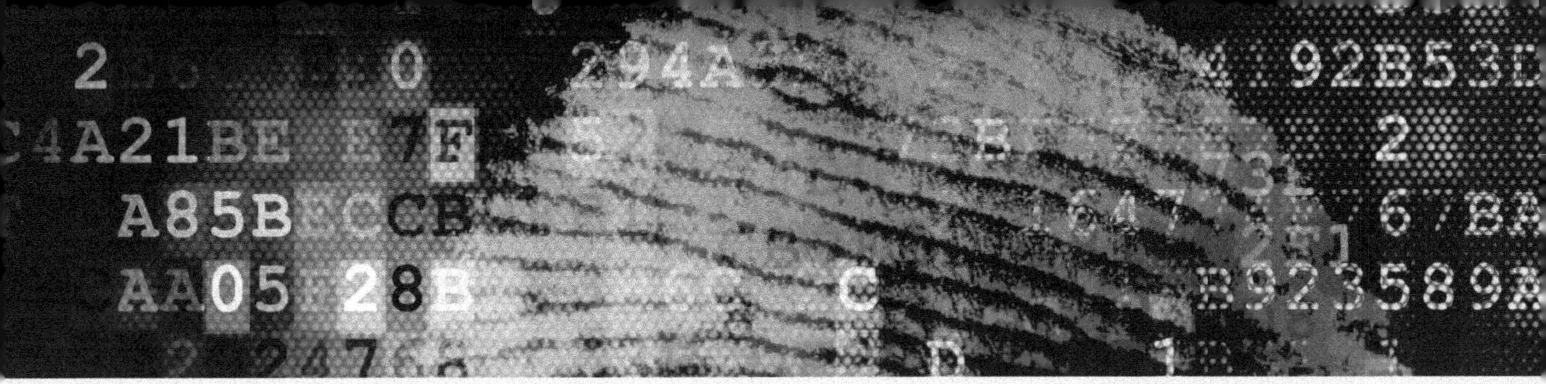

Decision-Making Criteria in the Justice Profession

6

While the structure of the American criminal justice system is easily identified, understanding its process is another matter. It is especially challenging to fully understand the application and impact of discretionary justice in its processes. As a concept, discretionary justice is often used to describe the operation of the American justice system because of its widespread use of discretion in its decision-making. The previous chapter discussed this challenge within a narrower context when it cautioned students of potential pitfalls surrounding their decision-making as future employees of the justice system. These decisions may at times be questioned and challenged by citizens who feel that as officials our decision to act or not act was improper. This may bring our decisions and actions into question as agency administrators and/or external agencies may decide to investigate the incident and the events leading to it.

All events leading to a complaint(s) against a justice official(s) begins with the suspects' initial contact with police. Once the police decide to arrest the suspect(s), they initiate the unfortunate journey through the justice system. The outcome of the case will eventually be subject to other discretionary judgments made by justice officials as the journey progresses. Since the ability to exercise discretion significantly defines our professional roles in the justice system, it is important to discuss criteria that we may use to reach these decisions.

To begin our discussion regarding decision-making criteria, let us distinguish between "formal" and "informal" decision-making. All justice officials make routine decisions based on standard operating procedures that are often supported by legal statutes and/or formal policies and procedures. For many agencies, these operating procedures formulate the foundation of their training curriculum. They are also likely to incorporate into their policies and training all procedures derived from U.S. Supreme Court case decisions related to agency practices. For justice officials, formal decisions are normally based on objective criteria because they adhere to written laws and supporting policy and procedure. This is likely to result in more transparent decisions. By comparison, justice officials also make informal decisions that are based on personal discretion. These types of decisions normally tend to be grounded on the officials' subjective interpretation of the situation that requires their decision. Since these are more subjective in nature they tend to lack full transparency. This does not necessarily make their practice wrong. Although many of these decisions routinely go unnoticed, the fact that they are often grounded on the person's professional judgment which is guided by their accumulated knowledge and work experiences underscore their importance (Samaha, 2006).

However, when the concept of "official authority" is combined with informal decision-making, this may at times complicate matters. For example, John Van Maanen's research (as cited in Samaha, 2006) of a police department revealed that officers tended to label citizens they interacted with into what may be considered unflattering categories. While this can simply be considered an interesting research finding, one must wonder how these perceptions are likely to influence the quality of interaction between criminal justice clients and justice officials?

Similar to police, all justice professionals perform their duties under some form of legal authority and in order for them to conduct these duties effectively, they need the public's support. This support may be offered in a variety of ways, however, no display of public support is greater than the *legitimacy* the public gives its justice officials. Through this legitimacy, the public recognizes, respects, and accepts the *authority* or *power* given to criminal justice professionals. Of their own free will, most citizens give these officials the authority to intrude in their personal lives. However, the public may also rescind this legitimacy as witnessed in countries known for corrupt criminal justice officials. This is especially true in countries where the public fears rather than respects its justice system. In these situations, it is difficult for the public to respect the authority or power of criminal justice officials. A main reason is that officials in these countries often base their work-related decisions on illegitimate criteria. For example, many years ago on one occasion a person traveling in a foreign country witnessed a police officer involved in a minor traffic accident in which the officer seemed to be at fault. His response to the other driver was, "I'll let you go this time, but next time I won't," and then drove away as the other driver was heard to say "but it was your fault". Another example also from many years ago involves a shared anecdote by a person from a foreign country who explained that on one occasion justice officials requested payment from a white-collar crime victim in order to officially act against the alleged perpetrator. Based on situations like these, we wonder how crime can be effectively controlled or prevented if the public fails to trust the authority of justice officials. The authors contend that it is difficult for a public to have confidence in agencies they distrust.

Regarding official decision-making within the justice system, Samaha (2006, p. 14) distinguishes between "legitimate" and "discriminatory decision-making criteria." This distinction forms the core of our discussion regarding professional decision-making by justice officials in the performance of their duties. When officials use legitimate criteria to generate on-the-job decisions, these decisions will most likely result in positive outcomes. The opposite is more likely to occur if officials rely on discriminatory criteria to formulate their decisions. For example, corrections officers are instructed to treat inmates with firmness and fairness. This means enforcing institutional rules equally to all inmates. The idea of treating all justice clients (suspects, defendants, convicted offenders, and victims) with fairness and respect is probably emphasized by staff training departments across criminal justice agencies. If this is true, then why does Samaha mention the existence of "discriminatory criteria" in justice decision-making? It seems that professional training should somehow effectively neutralize this problem. The answer may be that discriminatory decision making criteria has historically been part of the American justice system regardless of training efforts to eradicate it. Allegations that this practice continues can be witnessed in the media. However, for analytical purposes, rather than consider this as a justice system issue, let us think of it as a personal issue. If criminal justice agency training officials discourage its use, but the use of illegitimate criteria by staff persists, then it would appear that its roots lie outside of training. This problem may reside more with the employee than the system. When justice officials use the race, age, gender, or social status of the offender or victim to reach on-the-job decisions they do so at their own peril. Citizen complaints are likely to negatively affect the official(s) in question and will most likely influence the publics' perception of the agency and the justice system in general. A major problem is that discriminatorily based decisions are often difficult to detect. For example, two police officers may enter a "high-crime" area that is heavily populated by a certain group. While one officer may become more vigilant and suspicious of behavior based on neighborhood crime rates, the other officer may do so in response to physical characteristics of the residents. The personal nature of this decision-making criteria makes it difficult to detect discriminatory practices in certain situations, however, suspicions may arise through behavioral patterns detected in reported incidents. These patterns may raise suspicions about officials and agencies involved in these questionable incidents. Another major problem may be an organizational secrecy surrounding these practices. If they continue over extended periods of time and ignored by agency administrations, they may become institutionalized and eventually form part of the normal agency work culture. If they remain undisturbed, these practices may eventually present serious legal and financial risks to the agency. Therefore, the authors' emphasize the importance of routinely using legitimate criteria when making on-the-job decisions. When done properly, this practice is likely to eliminate many potential problems. Since coming in contact with the public should be based on legitimate reasons, officials should be able to objectively justify actions to be taken against a person. If the actions cannot be objectively justified, it might be advisable to consider other options. We are reminded that unwise decisions may result in detrimental consequences for all involved. These consequences may result in long term effects on professional careers. It is therefore advisable that we as justice officials reflect on our personal and social views regarding those who are different from us and to consider how these differences may influence our professional decisions. Incorporating the use of legitimate criteria to one's routine professional decision-making is likely to increase our professional tolerance when dealing with justice clients. This is not to suggest that justice officials become morally accepting of "deviant behaviors" displayed by average citizens. It simply means that justice officials should base their on-the-job decisions on objective criteria.

Student Self-reflection: This chapter discusses positive and negative elements of individual decision-making. The authors' advice is easily summarized—make professional decisions based on objective and legitimate information. Using transparent objective information based on agency protocols can help protect officials from civil and or criminal liability. To reinforce this concept, students should complete the attached self-reflection exercise. However, read this chapter carefully before participating in this exercise and remember the following:

1. Demonstrate your professional behavior by being thoroughly prepared for meetings.
2. Do not waste your supervisor's time by being unprepared for a scheduled meeting.
3. Remember that maximizing the effectiveness of a meeting means minimizing the time you speak and maximizing the time you listen. Listening is an acquired skill that should not be confused with hearing.

Self-Reflection Assignment Seven: The Mind-Mapping Process

As discussed in the previous assignment, all justice officials encounter work situations that require application of effective problem-solving abilities. More than one problem often exists within these situations with varying degrees of seriousness. To complicate matters, these problems may also be interrelated. The lesser serious problems that routinely surface from normal work activities require less complex responses. Because they routinely occur, officials may create guidelines that standardize their responses to these problems—often forming part of the agency's training curriculum. The use of guidelines allows sufficient flexibility when applying solutions to problems that while not identical they help maintain a similar rhythm. The more serious problems occur less often and most likely require a complex and customized solution. As a result, it is difficult to formulate a standardized approach to these unique and often unexpected situations. While it does not prescribe procedures to solve these problems, this assignment focuses on their analysis. Sometimes larger organizations (to which individual agencies belong) encounter problem situations that may require system-wide responses (e.g. problems that affect a state prison system, state juvenile correctional system, state parole system, municipal and state police departments, etc.). Because of the required far-reaching response, affected organizations must often implement a "paradigm" shift necessary to accomplish the necessary major changes. The purpose of this exercise is to assist internship students to critically analyze these potential situations. To complete the assignment, the student should make arrangements to interview an administrator from the agency where the student is interning. Since administrators are often busy, this meeting should be brief and probably not exceed 20 minutes. First, during the meeting the student should ask the administrator if they have ever experienced or participated in responding to a work situation that created a "very" serious problem(s) for the agency. If not, students should then ask them if they have known of a problem situation of this level that took place within their profession. Once they describe a situation write its summary in the center of the mind map provided below. Second, ask them what they believe should be the eight most important steps in response to fixing the situation. Ask them to prioritize the steps (ranking them from 1 meaning most important to 8 meaning the least important). Write these steps in the blocks surrounding the situation summary. Finally, write your opinion evaluating the supervisor's response and incorporate your own ideas regarding what you would have done.

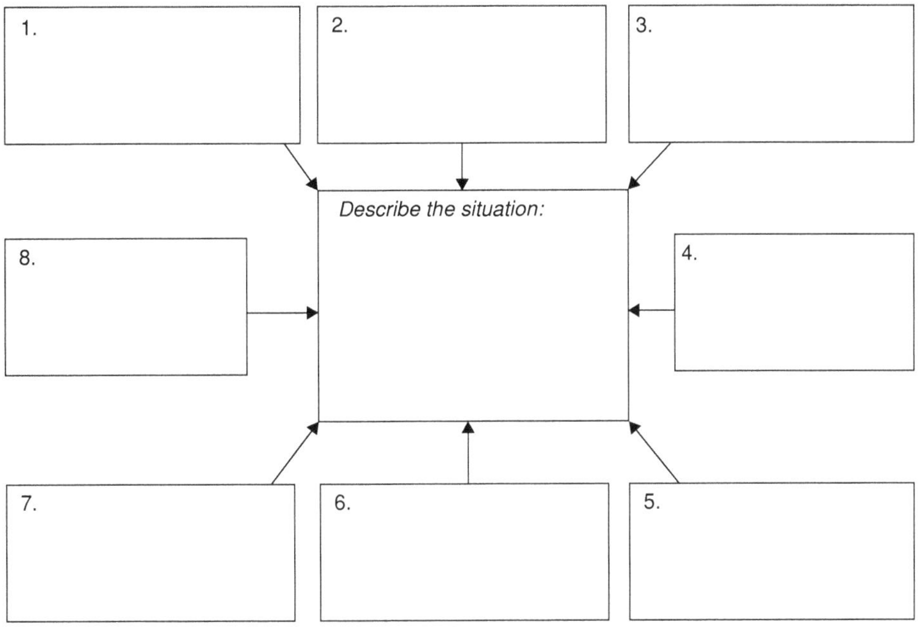

In the space provided below, write your opinion regarding the supervisor's response and incorporate your own ideas regarding what you would have done.

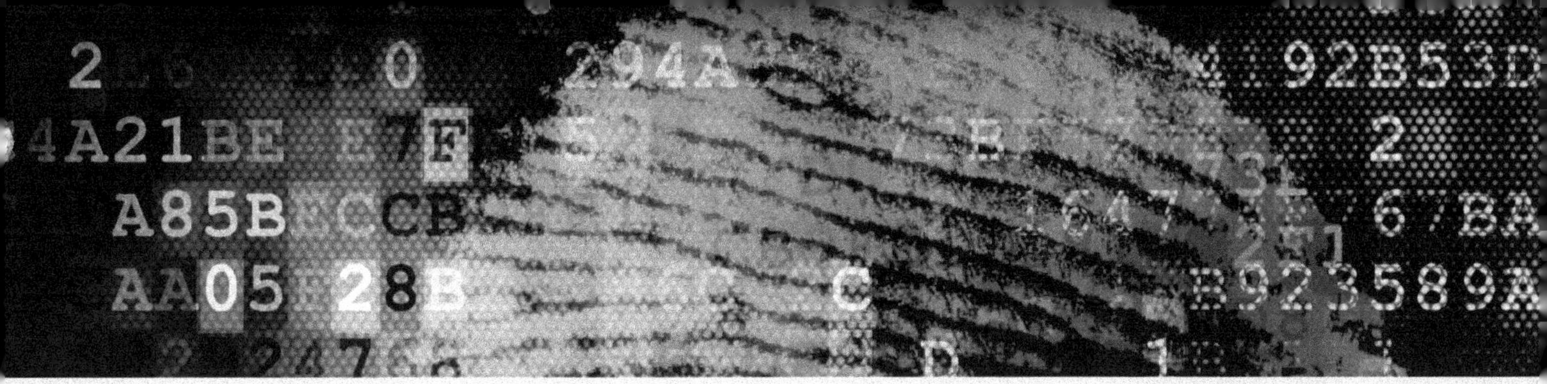

Skill-Building through the Agency Internship Experience

7

On its surface, an internship course appears to simply offer practical employment experience opportunities for criminal justice or criminology students. While it is true that the course exposes students to valuable hands-on experiences, these experiences can also be used to create broader learning opportunities. One way to do this is to identify one's own work-related skills that can be applied in this practical work setting and attempt to merge them with the professional skills being learned in the internship course. For example, the previous chapter and other sections of this book discuss the importance of "decision-making" in the justice profession. The ability to make sound professional decisions is in itself a skill. The authors would argue that, as a skill, proper decision-making transcends all other skills discussed in this chapter. Figure 7.1 depicts how decision-making skills may be strengthened by possessing other abilities. In other words, the ability to make effective professional decisions does not occur in a vacuum. Possessing the skills and abilities to properly

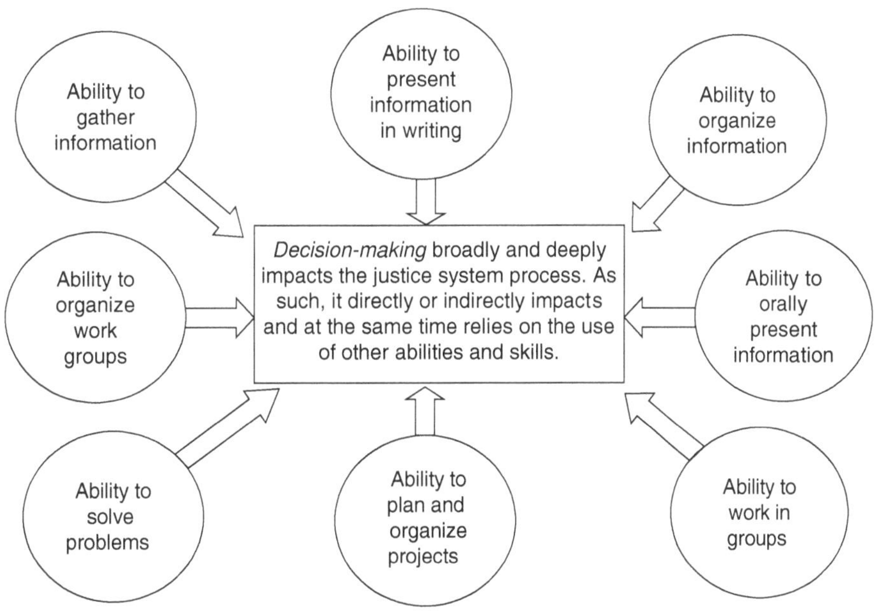

Figure 7.1 Important Criminal Justice Profession-Related Skills and Abilities

gather information; to organize and work effectively in groups; to organize, write, and clearly present information; to think critically and objectively in order to solve agency and personnel issues; and to be able to plan, organize, and effectively direct projects will all enhance our ability to reach better professional decisions.

The justice system primarily consists of a series of decision making points regarding the "processing" of clients (suspects, defendants, or correctional clients). Much of this process is dedicated to gathering information about the clients and persons connected to the client and their alleged offense (e.g., co-defendants, victims, witnesses, and other persons who contribute to the justice process). Depending on the responsibilities of the justice agency, this information is then used by officials for various purposes. Regardless of its application, the gathering and use of information plays a critical role in the justice process. It offers knowledge that is used by justice officials to make informed decisions regarding alleged and convicted offenders and criminal justice policy and practice. However, this information has a dual effect. First, it offers an awareness of benefits and potential issues and problems to justice officials. These are situations that the information allows administrators to detect. For example, it allows officials to identify questionable agency practices (e.g., patterns of excessive force, potential biases in treatment of clients or employees, and/or improper use of resources). This list can be quite extensive. Second, the information may not explain why these issues exist and therefore fails to explain why these patterns occur. Sometimes these unexplained situations may present more problems than those that information actually exposes. In summary, gathering information is one of the most important practices in the criminal justice professions. The proper application of this information in the various justice processes is equally important. However, all information gathered has its limits. Therefore, caution is advised when interpreting any gathered information. The following discussion focuses on the gathering, organizing, using, and presenting of information as part of sharpening and developing professional skills.

Developing the Ability to Gather Information: Becoming an effective criminal justice professional requires that we (1) be familiar with agency operational procedures; (2) be familiar with information gathered by the agency and the sources from which the information is attained and stored; (3) learning to properly use the information in the daily operations of the agency; and (4) learning to use this information to improve agency operations and solve problems identified by agency administrators.

An example of the use of information on professional decision-making:

On one occasion an experienced prison official said that while walking down a prison hallway during the institutions' inmate meal time, he could mentally select an inmate who was waiting in line to eat and then look at the time on his watch. Upon his return from whatever he was there to do, he could check his watch and calculate the inmate's waiting time in line. If the inmate's progress appeared too slow, this might indicate a potential inmate crowding issue. At this point he could contact the research staff and request an official inmate population analysis. In summary, this official's example met three important criteria regarding the gathering of information and decision-making. First, he was familiar with agency operations. Second, he objectively collected (in this case anecdotal) information. And third, he would use his agency research personnel to objectively evaluate his observations. If confirmed, he could then use this information to diagnose a potential operational problem and apply an administrative remedy.

The majority of the information gathered by agencies is usually in raw form (e.g., arrest reports, incident reports, presentence investigation reports, inmate disciplinary reports, agency memorandums). This list can also be very extensive. If extracted and properly organized, these documents can provide an important information base that, in turn, can be used to make important administrative decisions. If permitted by the agency, internship students should take time to examine the contents of some of these documents to better understand the value and potential application of this information. Knowing how and where to find information is an important part of making decisions in criminal justice. Although these documents may not have been originally designed to answer particular administrative questions, relevant information may be hidden within them. In these situations, critical thinking and diligence may prove to be useful. These are two skills/abilities that internship students should attempt to sharpen.

Developing the Ability to Organize Information: Gathering information is not the same as organizing it. These are two related but distinct processes that need to be discussed separately. As discussed earlier, justice officials routinely gather information to determine appropriate official dispositions (e.g., information related to the specifics of the offense(s) committed; the seriousness of the crime(s) committed by the client; or social and personal information about the offender(s)). Officials may then select and organize information from within these documents in specific styles. This information may now be helpful in understanding particular issues or problems. Inclusively, analysis of this information in an aggregate form (same information collected across many clients, incidents, and/or practices) helps officials and the public to better understand how the agency operates and assists evaluating how well it meets its mission(s), goals, and objectives.

Student interns should therefore become well acquainted with the official use of agency information. This can be easily done since much of these data are gathered based on existing and often written standard operating procedures. This information is gathered mostly for specific purposes such as determining the disposition of a case and its intended use is therefore somewhat narrow. However, the aggregate use of this information is not normally an intended application by agencies. Learning how to glean information for purposes such as evaluating agency practices or broader agency applications requires an ability to think analytically. Therefore, when administrators ask their staff to use this information for organizational assessment or evaluation, employees should ask for specific and clear guidance of the project before gathering any information. Sometimes administrators have a general idea of what they want but are unsure of the details. It may well be that they do not know what they are searching for until they see it. Therefore, staff conducting the actual research should ask as many questions as necessary to clarify the purpose of the project. The authors suggest that at this stage of the project, those conducting the actual research need to primarily ask questions and intently listen to the responses making sure to write all pertinent information. When all seems clear to the researcher, the specifics of the project request should be confirmed with the administrator who made the original request. At this time, the researcher could provide all necessary recommendations.

Searching for information may start with a bifurcated process. First, established agency information sources can be identified and reviewed for application to the project. Second, employees familiar with the agency may be contacted and queried about the availability of other less well-known information sources (e.g., annual reports from other related agencies and/or internal official memorandums). The project can be thought of as a journey and the stated purpose of the project is the final destination. If the purpose is not clearly identified the researcher(s) is likely to meander through the journey or process. This creates unnecessary obstacles to the successful completion of the project and meeting the administration's needs. Having a clear purpose increases the probability that the appropriate information can be gathered and the best method can be used for organizing the information.

Developing the Ability to Present Information in Writing: Many years ago a newly hired research assistant employed by a criminal justice agency was given the task of writing a report for the agency's chief executive. Fortunately for the research assistant, a mid-level administrator prevented the report from reaching the "boss's" desk. He returned the report back to the author and in a kind and professional manner made it clear that the report was intended for an administrator and not for a college professor. The research assistant was then given guidelines for writing the report. The report was rewritten and resubmitted without further concern. Two important lessons surface from this experience. First, student interns should become acquainted with the writing style normally used within the agency (e.g., formatting and writing memorandums, reports, and documents). Second, students should learn to identify the audience for whom the document is written. When the opportunity arises, student interns should inquire about these agency practices and preferences.

As part of an earlier discussion regarding decision-making in the justice system, the authors cautioned the reader that certain decisions could encounter legal challenges. It is in these situations that decisions based on acceptable established agency practices accompanied with well written and clear documentation of what transpired becomes important. As an extension of the legal process, related documents may become part of the litigation and therefore made public. This may include internal agency documents. What is written, and how it is written, may eventually reflect on the agency and its employees. Other than for litigation purposes, copies of these documents may be requested by sources outside the agency for multiple reasons. In conclusion, student interns should invest time and energy to developing strong writing communication skills required to properly prepare written information for agencies.

Developing the Ability to Orally Present Information: The thought of public speaking makes many people nervous. However, as long as it does not paralyze us, a little anxiety can actually help us improve our public speaking skills. This is an example of the so-called good stress. When the opportunity arises, student interns should practice engaging in information sharing sessions with agency administrators. One should attempt to maximize their internship experiences. This experience is especially rewarding if the information sharing occurs in a group setting. Receiving feedback from a number of people is always more enriching than receiving it from a single person. Students should remember that as interns they have only one reputation to establish. Interacting and sharing work-related information with other agency employees is part of the daily experiences in criminal justice agencies. Whether this is done on an individual basis or part of group meetings, this in part is how professional reputations are established. The authors suggest that students consider the following guidelines when participating in this process with co-workers and administrators. These guidelines may apply to both inter-individual and group meetings.

1. Prepare and organize materials to be discussed in advance. Although administrators may not expect student interns to memorize the information, they are expected to communicate it accurately. Therefore, students should be precise when preparing information for discussion. The clearer it is written, the easier it is to refer to it.
2. Anticipate and prepare for questions. On one occasion during a meeting with a number of administrators, a research assistant, who believing he had prepared well for the meeting, informed the group of a potential administrative problem. Without hesitation, the person

directing the meeting responded that awareness of the problem was insufficient—that what was needed was a proposed solution. At that point, the research assistant realized that he had not properly prepared for the meeting. He realized that stating the problem should have been accompanied by a plausible solution. Even if the proposed solution had not been adopted, this would have directed the discussion to exploring possible solutions.

3. Prepare a written agenda outlining the information in a logical order and be as brief as possible.
4. When organizing a presentation, allow a predetermined time limit for each topic to be discussed. The same guidelines should be used when using presentation software such as PowerPoint™. However, remember that technology is merely a tool that should be used to enhance the effectiveness of the presentation. When using technology a balance should be maintained between the presenter, the technology and the audience.
5. When possible and appropriate the presenter may propose solutions to problems.

Developing the Ability to Organize Work Groups: A significant amount of work in criminal justice agencies is performed by groups of employees. It has been said that a group of individuals working together are likely to develop better solutions to problems than a single individual—regardless of the person's level of education. However, this depends on the quality of employees and the manner of group interaction. For some people, group work means dividing the work among its members and eventually merging each portion into the main project. This usually proves to be insufficient. More detailed coordination is normally required.

Let us remember that the process used for fulfilling an agency's day to day obligations is different from that of solving its problems. Since groups are often used in performing the latter, it is important to discuss the dynamics of "problem-solving groups." First, members in these groups are usually persons who have a stake in solving the problem. This means that the solution is likely to somehow benefit their professional responsibilities. Because they are stakeholders in the process, personal agendas may form part of the group dynamics. This agenda may either be explicit or be implied. Second, these individualized agendas may result in disagreements or conflicts as the group engages in outlining potential responses to the problem. To serve as members of these groups or guiding them means, we need to understand how these groups operate. Therefore, the authors recommend the following guidelines.

First, selecting the group members is very important. Administrators understand that the quality of employees selected is a key ingredient to the success of their agencies. This means that if employees wish to be chosen to serve in problem-solving teams, they must prove to supervisors and administrators that they are capable employees. This usually means being a consistently responsible employee. Normally, we are not judged to be good employees by telling administrators that we are one—this is an earned reputation that is based on our past performance. Second, it is important for all group members to feel that they are a valuable part of the process. This means giving everyone an opportunity to participate and preventing members from dominating group meetings by controlling the group conversation. Giving others an opportunity to share their ideas and being open to their suggestions is beneficial to the group's success. Third, during its initial meetings, it is important to define and clarify each member's role. In addition, outlining the group's goals; the approximate number of meetings to be held and their dates, times, and duration of the meetings; the structure of written agendas for each meeting; and how work product is expected to be written, structured, reviewed, and rewritten when needed should all be stated in writing. Keep in mind that much of these expectations is flexible and should be amended as needed.

Developing the Ability to Work in Groups: A major obstacle to effectively working in groups is often our own personality. Some have compared our ability to control our ego to trying to hold an inflated beach ball underwater. No matter how much we try to hold it there, it will eventually surface. Whether it is strong, controlled, or weak, we all bring our egos to our jobs. This is especially apparent during group meetings where discussions often lead to disagreements and conflicting ideas. These conflicts and personality clashes are normal. Remember that group members are likely to have a stake in the group process, thus making disagreements inevitable. When we invest deeply in a process our internal work standards (a feeling of when we know our work quality meets our highest personal standards) have a tendency to intensify. These standards often help us determine if our work is "good" or "questionable." When asked to participate in these work groups, a strong personality can be a positive force in producing good work. Pride in our work can be an effective motivator. However, if allowed to go unchecked, it can alienate others and diminish the work product. Some of this can be avoided by the group's ability to establish clear guidelines intended to control dominant personalities and allowing weaker ones to flourish.

Developing the Ability to Plan and Organize Projects: All work assignments are time sensitive and need some degree of planning, regardless of the task complexity. Reduced to its basic elements, two questions need to be answered before starting work on an assigned work project. First, is the purpose of the assignment clear? Many years ago, during a conversation regarding personal experiences of being raised in a farming community, a discussant attempted to combine humor with his personal experiences. He went on to say that when his father was teaching him how to plow a field using a horse-drawn plow he was instructed to identify an object at the end of the field and direct the plow animals to that object as they pulled the plow. Doing so would most likely result in a straight row. The punch line to his story was that the first time he did this he unfortunately chose a cow as that object at the end of the field. One can only imagine the crookedness of a field row while trying to chase a cow with a horse and plow. Similar to choosing a stationary object at the end of that field, the purpose of a project has to be clarified to guide the necessary steps that will successfully complete the project. If not, constant changes will result in wasted time, energy, and work. This confusion is also likely to impact professional reputations. Remember that sometimes administrators have a general idea of what they want. Asking them clarifying questions can help them better understand what they are searching for and in the process prevent certain problems from surfacing. The second question is: Is there a project completion due date and is it known during the planning phase? If the due date is flexible, a reasonable date for completing the project should be established. If a due date is set, plans should be made to work within the permitted time frame. Once the assignment purpose and due date are established, the assignment planning phase begins. To do so, the project may be divided in logical steps and an attempt should be made to calculate the time that it takes to complete each step. When identifying the steps or phases necessary to complete the assignment, consider the process as a path that is composed of logically organized sequential steps. It is important to understand that the sequence sometimes does not permit starting a particular step without completing another. This can directly impact the completion date if complications occur in one step. For example, a gathering information step can be delayed if the request for that information was not properly submitted. In this case, the project cannot move forward until this request is submitted and approved. A proven effective planning method is the use of a Gantt chart for coordinating project activities. According to Houston (1999), "the Gantt chart, developed by Henry L. Gantt, is essentially a bar graph that shows the time allotment on a horizontal axis and the scheduled resource on the vertical axis" (p. 237). This chart serves as a tool for scheduling activities that Houston describes as "offering an overview of what tasks are to be completed, when they are to be completed, who is to work on them, and what, if any, resources can be used" (p. 237). Once the planning phase is complete, the supervisor(s) should be given a written copy of the plan to include, if any, Gantt charts associated with the project. Once approved, the project may be initiated. Students should not underestimate the importance of planning when carrying out work responsibilities. Developing this work habit may enhance an employee's professional reputation.

Developing the Ability to Solve Problems is one of the most important skills that students can develop. Rather than being a specific skill, this is mostly a combination of all the skills discussed above. These include, but are not limited to gathering, organizing and presenting (written and oral) information, organizing work groups, working effectively in groups, and planning and organizing projects designed to solve or address administration issues and problems. The successful application of these skills requires the knowledge of the skill and the appropriate application of the skill. Employees are most likely to succeed if they:

- Demonstrate *respect for the knowledge and experience of those who work for the* agency.
- Respect the knowledge and experience of agency employees by *listening* to them.
- As a practice, *listening should dominate speaking.* Listen and *glean useful and applicable information.*
- Be *respectful of authority. Avoid confrontational disagreements* they are more harmful than productive.
- When interacting with agency employees and supervisors, *be attentive and not dismissive.*

For students who wish to search for a proven problem-solving technique, a basic process can be found in most social science research methodologies. This is a good example of connecting academic instruction with practical agency operations. The process can be used to (1) search for answers to agency-related problems and (2) evaluate agency policies and practices. Most issues and problems arising from daily work routines are for the most part easily resolved by consulting the agency's written policies and procedures. If the answers are not found in an interpretation of existing policies and the issue or problem continues to reoccur, then a proposed policy resolving the matter is likely to be drafted and adopted by the agency. However, since their inception, the nature of justice-related agencies has been to continuously improve their operations in response to constantly increasing public demands on agency responsibilities and operating standards. For those who have experienced justice agency work, it often feels like the on-the-job demands increase at a faster pace than increases of additional resources. It is these constantly evolving standards that have created a greater demand on the quality of criminal justice employees. As the agencies' most valuable future assets, criminal justice and criminology students should ready themselves to be effective problem-solvers as they prepare to enter their criminal justice profession.

This employee quality becomes especially important when agencies are confronted with problems and issues that extend beyond the daily routine decision-making and whose answers are normally found in existing policy and procedures. As stated earlier, these broader problems and issues that lie outside the daily work routines are often demanded by forces external to the agency. These forces may include legislatures in search of public accountability, required agency changes resulting from lawsuits, or proactive administrations that wish to improve agency operations. These situations often lead agencies to hire the services of expert consultants. However, by possessing certain basic skills employees can either solve some of these problems or assist hired consultants to solve them.

When person(s) use this approach to resolve an issue or problem, it is important they put aside any preconceived notions as to what the solution should be. The information gathered should be permitted to guide any proposed solutions. Remember that a search for answers to these questions or issues originates with the basic premise that agencies search for "what is" not what "ought to be." If we decide to manipulate the information to simply support our preconceived solution that we pursue, why should we even go through the process? Administrative decisions should be based on some reasonably objectively acquired information.

It is suggested that the student refers to a social science research methods text to assist them in applying the scientific method as outlined below. When applying this problem-solving method to administrative issues remember that it is not a rigid process bound by strict rules. The ability to incorporate additional steps or remove others from the process increases its adaptability to a variety of problems. The important point to remember is that we are searching for a solution to complex problems utilizing an objective and proven method.

If closely examined, students will discover that this method integrates many of the skills discussed to this point. The methodology presented below is an outline of the suggested problem-solving process.

First, the process requires that the problem or issue be clearly understood by all involved. The best way to prove that it is clearly understood is to state it clearly in writing and ask everyone involved in the process to review it. To insure that the problem is clearly understood by those involved, it is suggested that the problem be written and reviewed by the participants in a question and answer session. There should be agreement in the group as to the stated problem.

Second, the group members should conduct a search for existing or published documents written by persons or agencies that confronted similar issues or problems. This search should include research on attempts made within the agency and an evaluation about why the previous efforts were unsuccessful or not implemented. A review of documents internal and external to the agency would most likely be of benefit to the group. Individual group members should participate in this document search. Among other benefits, it may offer a history of similar administrative problems or issues and their impact on agency operations; it may offer descriptions of methods used by previous administrators to study the problem or issue; and it may provide information regarding the success and failures of applied solutions. This information should be shared by the group members.

Third, based on the previous steps, the group should decide which information is helpful in identifying possible solutions and further decide whether more information should be gathered. This may require reviewing internal documents such as memorandums and reports. It is important to evaluate the information to determine whether the information is relevant to the problem or issue identified in the first step. If necessary, other information gathering methods may be used (such as interviewing individuals or sending written surveys to individuals who may have direct knowledge of the issue or problem). Whatever the method used, all questions asked of people should be directly related to the issue or problem clarified in the first step.

Fourth, the group should discuss whether there is a solution within the information discovered or whether the information leads the group towards finding a solution that might be unique to the agency.

Fifth, the group may compile a list of solutions or strategies that may be considered in solving the problem as stated in the first step.

Six, has agreement been reached in consensus as to the groups' conclusions?

Seventh, can a report be written that coherently explains the groups' decision that includes all the rationale for arriving at the decision?

In summary, this chapter briefly discusses a number of skills and abilities that when sharpened may help criminal justice and criminology students become more productive and potentially effective agency employees in the near future. However, the authors offer them as recommended guidelines and believe that they can serve as a foundation for furthering one's professionalism. The degree of success is contingent on a person's individual strengths, abilities, and efforts. These may include but are not limited to the level of personal commitment to the profession and personal internal standards that allows them to recognize if they have done or are doing their best work, if there is reason to have pride in their work, if they are unwilling to compromise the quality of the assignments given them, the level of insight they have when analyzing particular situations, and if they refuse to compromise their professional integrity. Successful careers often require strengthening the professional relationship between staff and agency. To enhance this relationship, we must be aware of the skills and abilities that agencies value in prospective employees. The development of skills and abilities can lend themselves to creating a more positive work environment which in turn can lead to greater career satisfaction (Payne, Blackwell, Collins and Carter, 2010). Completing the following self-reflection exercise may help students better understand this last statement.

Self-Reflection Assignment Eight: Self-Reflecting through Identifying Workplace Skills and Abilities

Students sometimes believe that once they receive a college degree, prospective employers are likely to extend them job offers because they now possess the academic credentials. In general, this is not necessarily the case. For most employment opportunities, a college degree is generally a requirement that allows applicants to compete for the position. In this regard, any academic credentials form part of a broader employment application. However, the contribution of a college degree to employment applications should not be underestimated. Review of an academic transcript may demonstrate the student's ability to initiate and complete long-term commitments. In addition, consistently earning passing and/or improving grades indicate the person's unwavering commitment to long-term goals by successfully meeting individual course objectives. Since course grades may be associated with class attendance, reading course assignments, writing detailed lecture notes, and actively participating in class activities, consistently earning "good" grades may reveal something about the applicant's work habits. But since this normally forms part of the employment application, applicants must somehow convince prospective employers that they possess the necessary attitude, skills, and abilities to perform the job requirements. For this reason, this assignment requires students to identify employee skills and abilities valued by the agency for which they are interning. To complete this assignment, students should schedule a brief meeting with their agency internship supervisor or their designee. Since administrators are often busy, this meeting should probably not exceed 20 minutes. Students should inform the supervisor or designee of the purpose for this interview when scheduling the meeting. During the interview, complete the assignment below.

Ask the person this question: Based on your experiences, what skills and abilities do you believe employees or prospective employees of this agency should possess in order to be professionally successful?
Your response:

On your own time (especially not during the meeting) and without discussing this with anyone, write the skills and abilities identified by the supervisor above that you possess.
Your response:

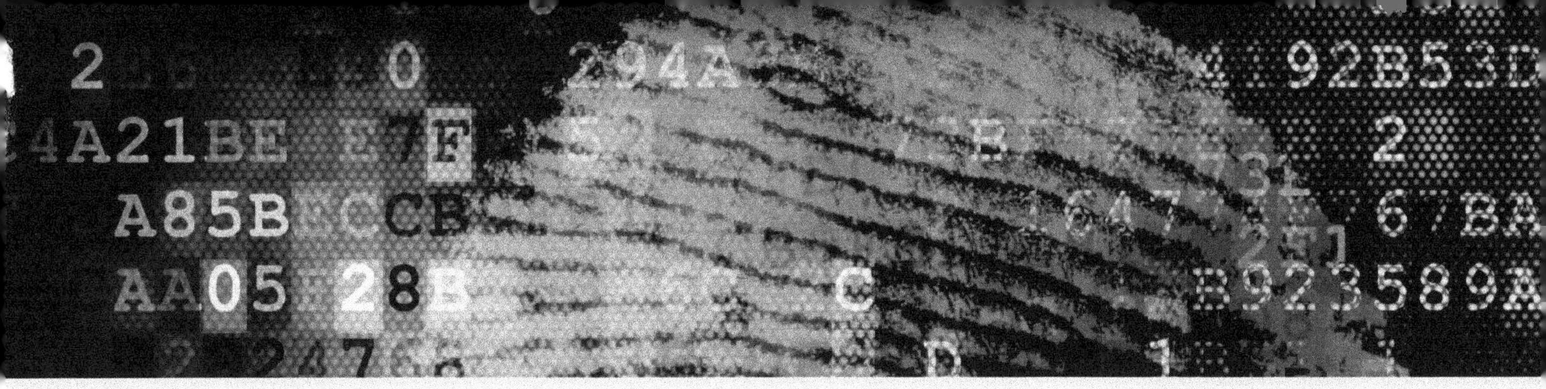

8 Summary and Conclusion

This text has been written for students enrolled in a criminal justice or criminology internship course. Its purpose is to prepare students for placement in a justice related agency and giving them an opportunity to apply their academic training to a professional setting. Although the text attempts to create a framework within which students can place their internship experiences, the success of the course ultimately rests with the students' motivation and commitment to the course. Its real value therefore lies in direct proportion to the investment students are willing to make to the course.

Placing the commitment issue aside, the text focuses on strengthening a student's ability to make appropriate professional decisions. Throughout the text, it is suggested that one must learn to, or sharpen the skills to listen, write, communicate, gather and organize information, and to identify and solve problems. The purpose is to help prepare students to meet the demands of the justice profession. To organize this process, the authors utilize routine interactions normally required of an internship course among the school's academic supervisor, the agency supervisor, and the student. These routine interactions occur throughout the duration of the course as students interact with professors responsible for directing and eventually submitting grades for the internship course and with agency supervisors who will guide and eventually evaluate the student's productivity. This text intensifies these interactions through a series of self-reflective exercises that bring the three parties closer together with the specific intent of strengthening these skills. This also allows students to explore career opportunities. This is something that all college and university students must eventually consider.

The internship course is one of various techniques that universities and colleges use to introduce employment or career experiences into the academic environment. Other available methods may include ride-along with police patrols; listening to and meeting guest speakers from justice professions; analyzing documentaries in the classroom; touring jails, prisons, and other justice-related institutions and organizations; or class assignments that send students to places outside the classroom where they witness and document real-life experiences (Payne, Sumter and Sun, 2003; Rockell, 2009). While all these methods share the common objective of bringing real-life experiences into the classroom, each has its own protocol. The authors encourage students to engage in as many academic opportunities that expose real-life criminal justice experiences as possible. They can only serve to learn more about the justice profession. However, the authors believe that the employment-like nature of internship experiences allow deeper insights into the justice professions.

For example, a portion of this internship guide focuses on the practice of decision-making in the justice system. When management authorizes employees to make decisions that significantly impact its organization, it trusts that employees will act responsibly and professionally. This trust carries with it the expectation that decisions and actions taken by employees will protect the integrity and dignity of the agency. However, a problem that is routinely confronted by criminal justice agencies is that they are often given increasing responsibilities with limited additional resources. It seems that they are often expected to do more with less. As a result, employees have become their most valuable resource. Therefore, criminal justice and criminology departments should do as much as possible to prepare students for the challenging careers in the justice professions that await them. It is insufficient for these institutions to award students a degree and simply expect them to learn the realities of criminal justice when they enter their profession. Rather than passing this responsibility to agencies, the learning process should begin in the classroom. Through this textbook, the authors attempt to contribute to this student preparation.

Although criminal justice and criminology students share the common goal of learning about crime and justice, they enter their academic discipline from diverse racial/ethnic and socioeconomic backgrounds. These backgrounds are composed of a combination of variables influenced by cultural experiences and socioeconomic levels and woven into individual personality traits and subsequent behaviors. The individual brings all of these elements into employment in the criminal justice system. It is therefore important that the students examine their own views and behavioral tendencies and use this self-knowledge when they begin their career path in the justice system. This self-appraisal will provide additional tools with which to make informed decisions as justice professionals. Organizing the internship experience so that students are able to learn the roles they might play in the justice system with opportunities for self-examination is the central premise of this text.

Self-Reflection Assignment Nine: Critical Thinking

This is a critical thinking exercise that attempts to focus on the student's ability to process information beyond its apparent meaning. Although the idea of thinking critically shares a common set of core values and seems to be a theme emphasized by many college and university settings the authors are not sure that all its proponents share specific meanings of how to apply it. However, debating its merits and identifying specific applications of critical thinking is beyond the scope of this exercise. At the risk of oversimplifying its application, for this particular exercise, the authors describe critical thinking as analyzing a criminal justice or criminology professional issue using objective elements of reasoning. First, any conclusion made regarding the issue should be based on open-minded reasoning that to the extent possible is absent of personal and socio-cultural biases. Second, the "Critical Thinking Community" (www.crticalthinking.org.pages/our-concpt-of-critical-thinking/4) argues that "critical thinking is self-directed, self-disciplined, self-monitored, and self-corrective thinking." Therefore, this exercise is solely based on the student's own objective manner of processing information and not on someone else's judgment. The authors hope that this exercise allows students an opportunity to sincerely focus inward and consider how their personal feelings may affect their judgment regarding criminal justice or criminology professional decisions. To do so, students should clearly identify, although not necessarily voice the elements that affect their reasoning. To conduct this exercise, students should do the following exercise:

*This internship experience clearly reflects materials you learned in your criminal justice and/or criminology courses. Check only one response.*_____ Yes _____No

In the space provided below, list specific reason(s) for your "yes" or "no" response.

In the space provided below, explain each of the reasons you listed above. Keep in mind that "critical thinking is self-directed, self-disciplined, self-monitored, and self-corrective thinking."

In the space provided below, clearly describe in what way the university/college could improve the internship course connection with the classroom instruction materials. Consider also, what the student can do to improve the connection. Again keep in mind that "critical thinking is self-directed, self-disciplined, self-monitored, and self-corrective thinking."

Self-Reflection Assignment Ten: The Internship Experience: A Search for Nexus

Completing this internship course should at a minimum accomplish four objectives. First, it should provide students with some knowledge about the practical operations of a justice-related agency and offer them insights into the relationship between the agency and the broader justice system. Second, it should demonstrate to students how their criminal justice and criminology course instruction materials are related to real-world experiences of the justice system. Third, through their internship experience, students should have the opportunity to apply and improve specific skills emphasized in classroom instruction. These include but are not limited to learning appropriate professional behavior and etiquette, learning to listen and to think critically, learning to gather and organize information, and learning to effectively communicate verbally and in writing. Finally, it should provide students with experiences that will help them select employment opportunities to jump-start their careers in the justice field.

This final exercise offers the student an opportunity to conduct a private self-examination regarding their internship experiences that may hopefully lead to self-improvement. As a private self-examination exercise, *the student should not feel compelled to share any of its information with anyone*. However, if they choose to do so, they may discuss some or all of this information with a professor. To explore experiences related to the objectives mentioned in the previous paragraph, this exercise is divided in two parts. First, it tries to assist students to identify specific internship experiences offered by the agency. Second, it asks for the meaning students give to their internship experiences as they relate to their professional expectations.

Instructions: Below is a listing of potential experiences you might have encountered during your internship.

> Note to the instructor: This is a private self-examination exercise intended to be used by the student as a self-improvement tool. The student should not be compelled directly or indirectly to share any portion of this information with anyone including university officials, instructors or agency officials. However, if students wish, they may discuss any portion of this exercise with a professor of their choice.

To the extent possible, please answer the following questions:

1. Did your work assignments keep you interested during your internship? If your answer to this question is yes, was your interest the result of your own initiative or the result of the effort made by the agency to provide a good learning experience for you? Explain. Write your answer to these questions in the space provided below. As part of your response, consider how this particular experience affects your professional development.

2. In the space provided below, describe the amount of effort you made to complete work assignments you were given.

3. In the space provided below, describe how you think the agency supervisor and others in the agency would describe your attire while you were on duty.

4. Regardless of the behavior of others in the agency, would you describe your own behavior while on duty as professional? Explain. Write your answer in the space provided below?

5. Interns will on occasions interact verbally with agency supervisors. Which of the following situations best describe the types of interaction you experienced? (Check as many as apply.)

_______ I was given instructions regarding my work responsibilities and assignments.
_______ I was asked to share information with my supervisor(s) regarding work assignments.
_______ I was asked to present information to a work related group of employees.
_______ Other. Explain:
____

In the space provided below, briefly describe how you would rate the quality of your interactions with agency supervisors?

6. Did you have occasion to provide written correspondence while working in this agency? If yes, please describe briefly:

In the space provided below briefly rate your ability to communicate (in writing) in these situations. Explain.

7. Did any new knowledge you acquired as a result of your internship contribute to your professional development? Explain. Write your answer in the space provided below.

8. Did experiences arising from your opportunities to work with agency officials and supervisors in this setting contribute to your professional development? How would you rate the quality of these experiences? Explain. Write your answer in the space provided below.

9. Did the supervisors in the agency provide you with a clear understanding of your work responsibilities and obligations? If yes, briefly explain in the space provided below.

If you were given a description of your responsibilities and obligations, in the space provided below explain if your duties coincided with the information given you by the agency supervisor(s)?

In the space provided below, describe how valuable this information was in relation to the work you performed.

10. In the prior statements you have been asked questions regarding your own professional development and motivation. These included motivation; personal initiative; professional appearance and behavior; oral and written communication; acquired knowledge; interpersonal skills; and roles, duties, learning objectives and professional responsibilities. Regarding this agency placement, what degree of professional behavior did you observe in others who work for the agency that would impact your future career? How did this experience influence your own attitude about how you might want to behave if you pursue this career? Explain. Write your answer in the space provided below.

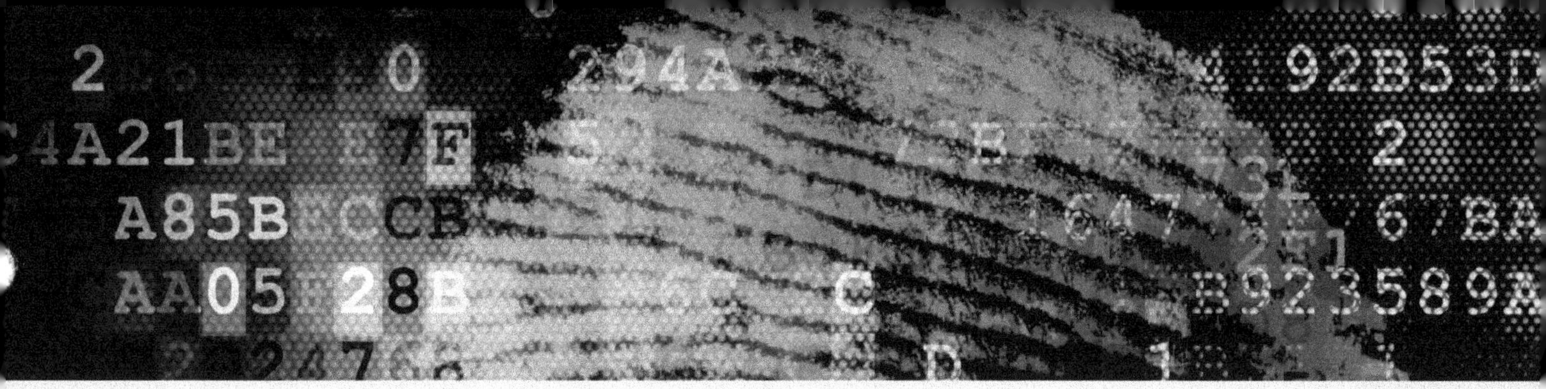

References

Bernard, T. J., Snipes, J. B., & Gerould, A. L. (2016). *Vold's theoretical criminology*. New York, NY: Oxford.

Chan, S. (2007, August 9). *The Abner Louima case: Ten years later*. Retrieved from http://cityroom.blogs.nytimes.com/2007/08/09/the-abner-louima-case-10-years-later/?_r=0

Cole, G. F., & Smith, C. E. (2004). *The American system of criminal justice*. Belmont, CA: Thompson-Wadsworth.

Daily Dunklin Democrat. (2013, August 8). *Dunklin County probation officer charged with corruption*. Retrieved from http://www.semissourian.com/story/1992271.html

Gaines, L. K., & Miller, R. L. (2014). *Criminal justice in action: The core*. Boston, MA: Wadsworth-Cengage Learning.

Diegelman, R. F. (1982). Federal financial assistance for crime control: Lessons of the LEAA experience. *Journal of Criminal Law and Criminology, 73*, 994–1011.

Gelb, M. J. (1998). *How to think like Leonardo da Vinci: Seven steps to genius every day*. New York, NY: Dell.

Gentry, J. W. (1990). What is experiential learning? In J. W. Gentry (Ed.), *Guide to business gaming and experiential learning* (pp. 9–20). American association for business simulation and experiential learning. Ann Arbor, MI: Nichols/GP Publishing.

Hagan, F. E. (2017). *Introduction to criminology: Theories, methods and criminal behavior*. Thousand Oaks, CA: Sage.

Hancock, B. W., & Sharp, P. M. (2000). *Criminal justice in America: Theory, practice and policy* (2nd ed.). New Jersey: Prentice-Hall.

Hirschinger-Blank, N., & Markowitz, M. W. (2006). An evaluation of a pilot service-learning course for criminal justice undergraduate students. *Journal of Criminal Justice Education*, *17*, 69–86.

Houston, J. G. (1999). *Correctional Management: Functions, skills, and systems* (2nd ed.). Chicago, IL: Nelson-Hall.

Marso, A., & Dean, R. (2013, October 18). *Supreme Court suspends Kline's Kansas law license. Disciplinary Administrator had argued for disbarment*. Retrieved from http://www.cjonline.com/news/2013-10-18/supreme-court-suspends-klines-kansas-law-license

Payne, B. K., Blackwell, B. S., Collins, C., & Carter, S. (2010). Exploring the ties between career satisfaction and education: Trait versus situational approaches. *Journal of Criminal Justice Education*, *21*, 77–90.

Payne, B. K., Sumter, M., & Sun, I. (2003). Bringing the field into the criminal justice classroom: Field trips, ride-alongs and guest speakers. *Journal of Criminal Justice Education*, *14*, 327–344.

Penn, E. B. (2003). Service-learning: A tool to enhance criminal justice. *Journal of Criminal Justice Education*, *14*, 371–383.

Prout, R.S. (1972). An analysis of associate degree programs in law enforcement. *Journal of Criminal Law, Criminology and Police Science, 63*, 585–592.

Samaha, J. (2006). *Criminal Justice*. (7th ed.). Belmont, CA: Thompson - Wadsworth.

Sgroi, C., & Ryniker, M. (2002). Preparing for the real world: A prelude to a fieldwork experience. *Journal of Criminal Justice Education*, *13*, 187–200.

Southerland, M. D., Merlo, A. V., Robinson, L. Benekos, P. J. and Albanese, J. S. (2007). Ensuring quality in criminal justice education: Academic standards and the reemergence of accreditation. *Journal of Criminal Justice Education*, *18,* 87–105.

St. Mary's University. (2016). *Undergraduate course catalog, 2016–2017 ed.* Retrieved from http://stmarytx.edu/undergraduate/course-descriptions/cj/

Stone, W. E., & McLaren, J. (1999). Assessing the undergraduate intern experience. *Journal of Criminal Justice Education*, *10*, 171–183.

Urbina, I., & Hamill, S. D. (2009, February 12). *Judge pleads guilty in scheme to jail youths for profit*. Retrieved from http://www.nytimes.com/2009/02/13/us/13judge.html?pagewanted=all

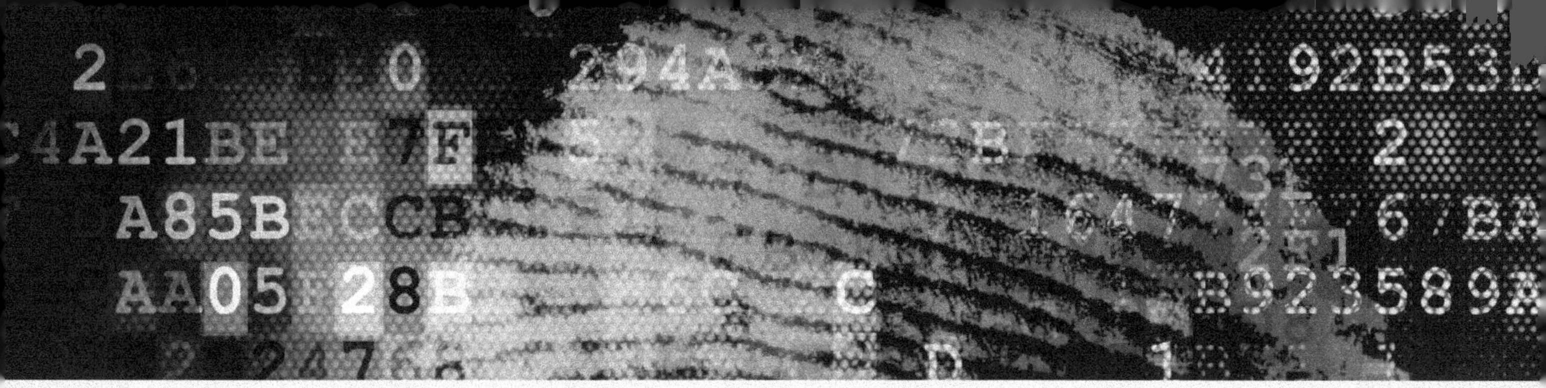

About the Authors

Pedro Lopez received his Ph.D. in criminal justice from Sam Houston State University. He served in various capacities for a major state correctional system and is currently an Associate Professor of Criminal Justice at St. Mary's University in San Antonio, Texas.

Armando J. Abney received his Ph.D. in sociology from the University of Notre Dame. He is currently an Associate Professor of Criminology and Sociology and is the Chairperson for the Department of Criminal Justice and Criminology at St. Mary's University in San Antonio, Texas. He has worked as a research methodologist for the Texas Department of Mental Health.

Patricio Jaramillo received his Ph.D. in Counseling Psychology from Arizona State University. He is Professor Emeritus in the Department of Education and served as the President of Student Services at the University of Texas at Permian Basin. Currently, he serves as an External Evaluator to grants awarded by the U.S. Department of Education for Bilingual/ESL programs and for Hispanic Serving Institutions.

www.ingramcontent.com/pod-product-compliance
Ingram Content Group UK Ltd.
Pitfield, Milton Keynes, MK11 3LW, UK
UKHW051330130926
15127UKWH00013B/96

9 781524 901554